ROUTLEDGE LIBRARY EDITIONS: PHONETICS AND PHONOLOGY

Volume 23

SONORITY CONSTRAINTS ON PROSODIC STRUCTURE

SONORITY CONSTRAINTS ON PROSODIC STRUCTURE

DRAGA ZEC

LONDON AND NEW YORK

First published in 1994 by Garland Publishing, Inc.

This edition first published in 2019
by Routledge
2 Park Square, Milton Park, Abingdon, Oxon OX14 4RN

and by Routledge
711 Third Avenue, New York, NY 10017

Routledge is an imprint of the Taylor & Francis Group, an informa business

© 1994 Draga Zec

All rights reserved. No part of this book may be reprinted or reproduced or utilised in any form or by any electronic, mechanical, or other means, now known or hereafter invented, including photocopying and recording, or in any information storage or retrieval system, without permission in writing from the publishers.

Trademark notice: Product or corporate names may be trademarks or registered trademarks, and are used only for identification and explanation without intent to infringe.

British Library Cataloguing in Publication Data
A catalogue record for this book is available from the British Library

ISBN: 978-1-138-60364-6 (Set)
ISBN: 978-0-429-43708-3 (Set) (ebk)
ISBN: 978-1-138-34687-1 (Volume 23) (hbk)
ISBN: 978-1-138-34689-5 (Volume 23) (pbk)
ISBN: 978-0-429-43716-8 (Volume 23) (ebk)

Publisher's Note
The publisher has gone to great lengths to ensure the quality of this reprint but points out that some imperfections in the original copies may be apparent.

Disclaimer
The publisher has made every effort to trace copyright holders and would welcome correspondence from those they have been unable to trace.

SONORITY CONSTRAINTS ON PROSODIC STRUCTURE

DRAGA ZEC

GARLAND PUBLISHING, Inc.
New York & London / 1994

Copyright © 1994 by Draga Zec
All rights reserved

Library of Congress Cataloging-in-Publication Data

Zec, Draga.
　Sonority constraints on prosodic structure / Draga Zec.
　　p.　cm. — (Outstanding dissertations in linguistics)
　Includes bibliographical references and index.
　ISBN 0-8153-1699-2
　1. Prosodic analysis (Linguistics).　2. Lexical phonology.
3. Lexical grammar.　I. Title. II. Series.
P224.Z43　1994
414'.6—dc20   94-1107
                                                              CIP

Contents

Preface		viii
1	**Introduction**	**3**
2	**Sonority Constraints on Moras**	**11**
	2.1 Introduction	11
	2.2 Asymmetries in the sonority of moras	12
	2.3 Type One (Syl ⊂ Mor = Seg)	17
	2.4 Type Two (Syl = Mor ⊂ Seg)	17
	2.5 Type Three (Syl ⊂ Mor ⊂ Seg)	18
	2.5.1 Danish	19
	2.5.2 Lithuanian	22
	2.5.2.1 Lexical Component	26
	2.5.2.2 Postlexical Component	32
	2.5.3 Kwakwala	32
	2.5.4 Italian	38
	2.6 Type Four (Syl = Mor = Seg)	40
	2.6.1 Imdlawn Tashlhiyt Berber	40
	2.7 Sonority of Moras and Sonority of Syllables	42
	2.8 Further Predictions	46
	2.8.1 Types of Closed Syllables	46
	2.8.2 Types of Heavy Syllables	49
	2.9 Comparison with the Onset/Rhyme Representation	52
	2.9.1 Tree Geometry	53
	2.9.2 Constraints	55
3	**Formation of Moraic and Syllabic Structure**	**62**

	3.1	Introduction 62
	3.2	Sonority 62
		3.2.1 Sonority Scales 62
		3.2.2 Universal and Language-Specific Sonority Ranking 65
		3.2.3 Relative Sonority Ranking 69
	3.3	Proposal 73
	3.4	Moraic and Syllabic Structure 77
		3.4.1 Morification 78
		3.4.2 Syllabification 81
	3.5	Consequences 84
		3.5.1 Sonority Sequencing Constraints and the Syllable Contact Law 84
		3.5.2 Minimal Distance Constraints 85

4 The Mora as a Prosodic Unit   89
  4.1 Introduction 89
  4.2 Bulgarian 'Liquid Metathesis' 90
  4.3 An Excursus into Bulgarian Phonology 92
  4.4 Epenthesis 98
  4.5 Formation of Prosodic Structure 100
      4.5.1 Cyclic Domain: Moras vs. Syllables . . . 100
      4.5.2 Postcyclic Lexical Domain 102
      4.5.3 Apparent Counterexamples 104
  4.6 Further Implications 106
  4.7 Implications for Prosodic Phonology 107

5 Case Study: Serbo-Croatian   112
  5.1 Introduction 112
  5.2 Presonorant Lengthening 115
      5.2.1 Yer Vowels 115
      5.2.2 The Conditioning Environment 118
  5.3 The Analysis 121
  5.4 The Accentual System 126
      5.4.1 Background Information 126
      5.4.2 Tone Linking Rule 130
  5.5 Underived Forms 135
      5.5.1 Nominal Stems 135
  5.6 Derived Forms 145
      5.6.1 Accented Suffixes 145
      5.6.2 Unaccented Suffixes 152

5.7	Adjectival Stems	156
5.8	Suffixes with Yers	165
5.9	Verbal Forms	171
5.10	Concluding Remarks	178

6 Consequences for Prosodic Phonology 184

Bibliography 190

Index 201

Preface

This study is my Stanford University Ph.D. dissertation, completed in 1988, and appears here with only minor revisions. The goal of this work is to establish correlations between the internal constituency of the syllable and the sonority of segments. Its major claim is that valid correlations can be established only under the moraic theory of syllable-internal structure. This work thus represents an argument for the moraic theory of the syllable.

While this study was in the making, the moraic theory of syllable-internal structure was relatively new, and its arboreal counterpart very much part of the current scene. Yet, within only a few years, the scene has changed considerably, with the moraic framework assuming a strong position in the field. This shift is due to the explanatory power and the parsimonious nature of the moraic framework itself, as well as to the role it played in the development of prosodic morphology. In sum, my general position on the value of this framework remains unaltered to the present date, although I have, naturally, changed my views on a number of smaller issues addressed in this work.

Completion of this work would not have been possible without help and encouragement from members of the Stanford community, among them Young-mee Yu Cho, Cleo Condoravdi, Kristin Hanson, Jeff Goldberg, Sharon Inkelas, K.P. Mohanan, John Stonham, and above all, the members of my dissertation committee, Paul Kiparsky, Joan Bresnan, Will Leben, and Bill Poser. I am also greatly indebted to Dikran Karagueuzian, as well as Antony Green, Michael Inman and Emma Pease, for their expert help in producing this book.

I dedicate this work to my parents, Ljubica and Slobodan Zec.

Sonority Constraints on Prosodic Structure

1
Introduction

The goal of this study is to argue for a prosodic hierarchy with the mora, rather than the syllable, as its lowest unit. First I will outline the theoretical assumptions of this study, and then follow up with a summary of its principal claims.

The general theoretical framework I assume here is that of lexical phonology and morphology (Kiparsky 1982a, 1982b, 1983, 1984, 1985, Mohanan 1982, 1986, Halle and Mohanan 1985). In most respects, my assumptions about this framework are fairly standard. The two major components are the lexical and the postlexical, with phonological rules applying in both; the lexical component, in its turn, may contain one or more levels. Originally, it was assumed that all lexical rules are cyclic, that is, that the lexical/postlexical division fully corresponds to the cyclic/postcyclic one. But as argued in Booij and Rubach 1984, this view is too strong. In order to account for a class of noncyclic rules that apply in the lexicon, following all cyclic rules, Booij and Rubach 1984 propose a postcyclic lexical level where the domain of rule application is the word (see also Booij and Rubach 1987). Under Booij and Rubach's proposal, noncyclic rule application is found only at those lexical levels at which no morphological rules apply, which ties up cyclicity with the mode of morphological derivation. A further development is found in Halle and Mohanan 1985: under this proposal, any lexical level can be either cyclic or noncyclic, regardless of whether it contains morphological rules or not.

Within this general framework is couched the prosodic structure, which I focus on in the second part of this book. The standard assumption about prosodic structure is that it consists of prosodic constituents whose property is to form a hierarchy, as in (1) (see Selkirk 1978, Nespor and Vogel 1982, 1986, Hayes 1989a):

(1) Prosodic Hierarchy
     phonological phrase
     phonological word
     foot
     syllable

Prosodic constituents are at least in part motivated by the fact that they function as domains of phonological rules. Note however that the constituents forming the prosodic hierarchy are of two kinds. Those like the phonological word and the phonological phrase are generated by virtue of a mapping from the morphosyntactic structure; the constituents at the lower end, the syllable and the foot, are constituted of phonological segments and their systematic groupings, and are independent of morphosyntactic structure. My focus will be on the lower end of the hierarchy. As I argue, this hierarchy needs to be enriched with one more unit — the mora, which I propose to add as its lowest constituent. This yields a new version of the hierarchy in (2):

(2) Prosodic Hierarchy (revised)
     ...
     foot
     syllable
     mora

Following up on certain other proposals of the same kind (Selkirk 1986, Inkelas 1987b), I will argue that the prosodic hierarchy needs to be divided up into two independent hierarchies, one consisting of the mora, syllable, and foot, and the other of the units above the foot.

The principles of prosodic phonology relevant in the present context are the Strict Layer Hypothesis (Selkirk 1984b), which ensures that each layer of prosodic constituents be properly included into the next higher one; and Itô's 1986 Principle of Prosodic Licensing, which assigns to prosodic structure the task of a general licenser of phonological structure. These two principles are given in (3) and (4):

Introduction

(3) *Strict Layer Hypothesis:* A category of level i in the hierarchy immediately dominates (a sequence of) categories at level $i - 1$. [Selkirk 1984b]

(4) *Prosodic Licensing:* Phonological units have to be incorporated into (higher) prosodic structure (modulo extraprosodicity). [Itô 1986]

Under the assumption that the prosodic phonology is couched within the general framework of lexical phonology and morphology, we will be able to identify in precise fashion the component, or the level, at which prosodic constituents are created. Given Itô's Principle, at least one prosodic constituent will have to be present from the earliest level of the lexical component, in order to provide prosodic licensing. And, given the Strict Layer Hypothesis, this constituent will have to be the lowest one in the hierarchy. With the revised version of the hierarchy in (2), it will be claimed that the mora is the only constituent that has to be present throughout the derivation. This will not be a necessary property of any of the higher up units, including the syllable.

With this theoretical background, we will now turn to a brief summary of the claims to be made in this study.

The arguments for the prosodic status of the mora are presented in two steps. First, I argue for the mora as a primitive subsyllabic constituent, that is, for the representation of subsyllabic structure in (5):

(5) a.

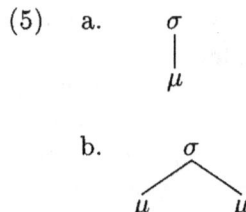

b.

This representation of subsyllabic structure has been proposed in Hyman 1985, and McCarthy and Prince 1986. The arguments presented in its support concern the tonal phenomena in the former case, and the properties of various prosodic templates in the latter. But while Hyman 1985 and McCarthy and Prince 1986 demonstrate that the notion of mora is necessary to express the generalizations pertaining both to tone and to prosodic templates, they do not show that the representation of subsyllabic structure in (5) is the only one capable of capturing the right generalizations. I bring in a new set of arguments which crucially choose between this and the other available representations of subsyllabic structure, those expressed in terms of the onset/rhyme constituents (see for example Selkirk 1982, Steriade 1982), or those that link the CV skeleton directly to the syllable node (as in Clements and Keyser 1983). As will be shown, the representation in (5) is the only one capable of capturing the sonority properties of subsyllabic constituents, which results in its ability to constrain the subsyllabic structure in a desirable fashion

Second, I argue that the mora is a prosodic constituent, and furthermore, that its presence in subsyllabic structure is a necessary prerequisite for its prosodicity.[1] The argument for the mora as a subsyllabic unit is developed in Chapters Two and Three; in Chapters Four, Five, and Six, I argue for the prosodic status of the mora

In Chapter Two it is shown that the sonority requirements on syllables are constrained at more than one level: at the level of the syllable and at the level of what is known to be the mora — either in the primitive or in the derived sense. While it is well known that syllabic segments, that is, those that can head the leftmost mora of a syllable, are a subset of the entire segment inventory, it is less known (and is argued for in this study) that segments heading the rightmost mora, henceforth moraic segments, are also a subset, potentially a proper subset, of the segment inventory. The membership of each of these subsets is determined on a language-particular basis, which argues for their relative independence. Although the two subsets stand in a fixed mutual relation — syllabic segments are always a subset of moraic segments — this subset relation follows as a necessary consequence of the representation in (5) (paired with subsyllabic metrical structure); thus the fact that the mutual relation of the two subsets is fixed is not at odds with the claim that the two subsets are independent of each other. In sum, the claim is that the relation between the various sets of segments is as in (6):

(6)   Syllabic $\subseteq$ Moraic $\subseteq$ Segment Inventory

Introduction 7

In order to show that (6) is a valid generalization, we show that (6) makes several correct predictions. First, this generalization sets the range of possible language types. Second, by virtue of (6) we can derive various implicational relations between types of closed syllables on the one hand, and types of heavy syllables on the other, including Trubetzkoy's generalization about the implicational relation between CVV and CVC syllables. Finally, it is argued that the representation with the mora as a primitive subsyllabic constituent fully captures the generalizations proposed in this chapter, which is not possible if moras are not part of the representation

In Chapter Three we take as a point of departure the claim about the primitive status of the mora, and propose two algorithms for building prosodic structure: one that creates moras, and one that groups moras into syllables. While the morification algorithm makes reference to the relative sonority of segments as well as to the minimal sonority imposed on moraic segments, the syllabification algorithm adheres to the principle of minimal sonority imposed on syllables, and to universal as well as language-specific principles of mora-to-syllable mapping. From this we derive both the curve-like sonority properties of the syllable, and the sonority constraints that hold between adjacent syllables

In Chapters Four and Five, I demonstrate that in some cases we need the presence of moras while explicitly requiring the absence of syllables, which crucially argues for positing moras not only as subsyllabic constituents but also as prosodic units. In Chapter Four I discuss certain phonological phenomena in Bulgarian, in particular the liquid epenthesis, which call for an early level in the lexical phonology with only moras but no syllables present. If prosodic units provide prosodic licensing, and if prosodic licensing is necessary at all stages of the derivation, then in the absence of syllables this role will have to be performed by some other prosodic units, and the best candidate for this is the mora. Chapter Five brings in evidence from Serbo-Croatian bearing on the prosodic status of the mora. As a pitch-accent language, Serbo-Croatian has a tone assignment rule which operates on syllables. This rule does not become available until Level Two of the lexical phonology; the reason for this, I claim, is that syllables are not formed before Level Two. At Level One only moras are operative, as evidenced by cases of compensatory lengthening in the environment of sonorants, which are found only at this level.

In the final chapter I explore further consequences of the prosodic status of the mora, pertaining to various prosodically driven types of behavior such as stress assignment and extrametricality, as well as to the general properties of weight phenomena.

Before closing this chapter, several residual issues need to be mentioned. First, a comment is in order regarding the representation of subsyllabic structure to be utilized here. (5) is only one of the representations with moras as primitives that have been proposed in the literature. The full range of proposals, taken from McCarthy and Prince 1986, is given in (7)-9:

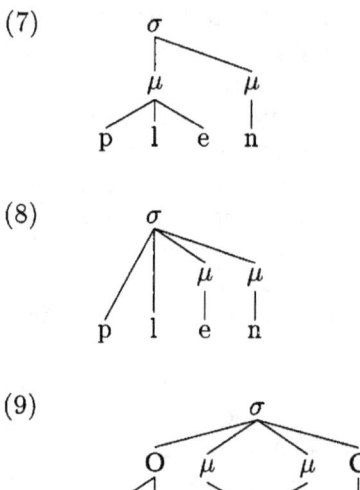

While all these representations are equally compatible with the claim that the mora is a primitive of subsyllabic structure, they are not all compatible with the claim that the mora is a prosodic constituent. Only (7) is compatible with this latter claim, given the Strict Layer Hypothesis, as well as the Principle of Prosodic Licensing, and this is my principal motive for adopting it here. In this case, all segments are included into constituents at the same prosodic level, that is, the level of the mora. In (8) some of the segments are included at the level of the mora, and others at the level of the syllable, which is inconsistent with the claims of the prosodic phonology.[2] And (9) is an inadequate representation because the subsyllabic prosodic level consists of nonuniform constituents, which again is not in the spirit of prosodic phonology.

Introduction

Second, by adopting the representation in (7) I am tacitly assuming that the onset/rhyme constituency is not necessary, and can therefore be dispensed with; this is in line with the proposal made in Clements and Keyser 1983. Most of the cases presented in Steriade 1988 as phonological evidence in favor of the rhyme constituent can be analyzed with equal success in terms of the representation in (7). For example, the conditions on *l* velarization in English can be restated in the following way: *l* is apical, that is, nonvelarized, if and only if it is immediately followed by a vowel. In all oher positions *l* is velarized, including any of the moraic positions, as well as syllable-final nonmoraic position. The case which presents a problem for the representation with moras as primitives is that of Chinese vowel backing; rather than address it here, I will leave this problem for future research.

Steriade's arguments for the rhyme constituent also open up the problem of onsets, which appear to function as constituents in speech errors, language games, and the alliteration patterns in poetry. This is further related to the representation of tautosyllabic geminates, which requires the onset constituent (to the extent that such representation is indeed needed). Although worthy in their own right, these issues will remain outside the scope of this study.

Notes

[1] Itô 1989 implicitly makes the claim that moras are prosodic constituents, by having what appears to be relatively late syllabification apply on morified structure.

[2] The representation in (8) is utilized in Hayes 1989b.

2
Sonority Constraints on Moras

2.1 Introduction

The aim of this chapter is to establish a set of parameters which would lead to a universal inventory of syllable types, as well as to implicational relations that might hold between them. In particular, I argue that, in addition to having sonority constraints on syllables, we also need to constrain the sonority of moras. I further argue that sonority requirements on moras, together with those on syllables, are essentially all we need to establish the right set of parameters: it will be shown how the proposed parameters derive possible types of closed syllables on the one hand, and of heavy syllables on the other.

Different frameworks express the notion of mora in different ways. With the onset/rhyme representation, given in (1), we arrive at the notion of mora by an interpretive procedure: the number of branches under the rhyme node corresponds to the number of moras that the syllable has.

(1)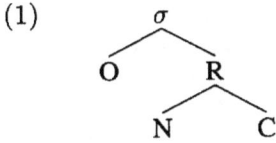

With the representation that incorporates the mora as a primitive of the structure, the number of moras within the syllable is, of course, computed in a much more straightforward fashion.

(2) a.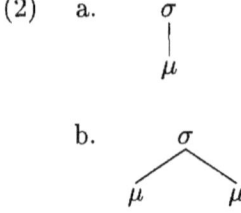

 b.

I will be utilizing here the representation of subsyllabic structure in (2), with moras as primitives, rather than the type of representation in (1), in which the mora is a derived notion. The choice may appear arbitrary, since none of the claims to be made in sections 2.2 through 2.6 argue for one of these representations over the other. However, the claims made in sections 2.7 to 2.9 crucially argue for a direct representation of moras in subsyllabic structure, that is, for selecting the representation in (2) over the representation in (1).

2.2 Asymmetries in the sonority of moras

Weight is one of the generally accepted properties of the syllable. If moras are taken to be units of weight, then a light syllable has one mora, as in (2)a, and a heavy syllable has two moras, as in (2)b. But a further important thing to be observed about the bimoraic syllable is that the two moras it contains exhibit systematic asymmetries in sonority requirements.[1] The second mora may be less sonorous than the first, as in (3), or it may be equally sonorous, as in (4).

(3)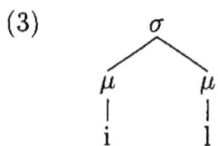

(4)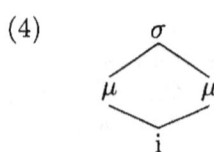

But it can never be *more* sonorous than the first one, as in the ill-formed (5):

(5)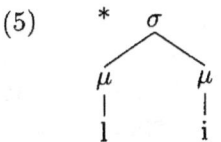

In one particular approach, notably that of Kiparsky 1979, 1981, these configurations are derived from subsyllabic metrical structure with universally specified node labeling. Later in this chapter I adopt the spirit of this proposal; thus I agree with the claim that such asymmetries eventually result from the internal organization of the syllable. But I also make a further claim: that the range within which the asymmetries are manifested is determined solely by the sonority requirements on moras, as proposed in Prince 1983:57-58, and this is what we now turn to. Before doing so, however, we will digress briefly to clarify a terminological point. I will henceforth refer to those segments that can 'license' the second mora of a heavy syllable as *moraic*; and to those that can 'license' the first mora of a heavy syllable, or the only mora of a light syllable, as *syllabic*. These segments will be the most sonorous segments under their respective moras.[2] We will see in a moment that syllabic and moraic segments form sets whose membership may vary from language to language, but whose mutual relation is fixed: the former is always a subset of the latter. This terminology is only descriptive; I explore the theoretical implications of the findings about the behavior of the two types of segments in sections 2.7-2.9 of the present chapter.

As has been often pointed out, the syllable forms a sonority curve, with one segment acting as the sonority peak, i.e. as the nucleus. I will assume here the sonority scale of the standard type, and will defer to the next chapter the question of how to encode degrees of sonority in the grammar. One version of such a scale is given in (6):[3]

(6) Sonority Scale
obstruents
nasals
liquids
vowels

Universally, segments occupying the sonorous end of the scale can act as syllable nuclei, while those occupying the nonsonorous end of the scale are less likely to perform this role. Of course, what segments will be syllabic is determined on a language-specific basis. For example, the set of segments that can act as syllable peaks in English is given in (7):[4]

(7) English syllabic segments:
     nasals
     liquids
     vowels

We can in fact say that the set of syllabic segments is always a subset of the entire set of segments.[5]

The segments listed in (7) are those which can occupy the first mora of a heavy syllable or the only mora of a light syllable. Note, however, that the requirements are much looser on the *second* mora of a heavy syllable. In English, any segment can appear in this position, which makes the set of English moraic segments coextensive with the entire set of segments:

(8) English moraic segments:
     obstruents
     nasals
     liquids
     vowels

Thus, the set of moraic segments, like the set of syllabic segments, is a subset of the segment inventory. Furthermore, in some languages the set of moraic segments can be a *proper* subset of the segment inventory. This situation is found at least in those languages in which CVV syllables act as heavy, and CVC as light (cf. McCarthy's 1979a, 1979b discussion of Tiberian Hebrew or Hayes' 1981, 1982 discussion of Yidin^y); only vowels appear to be moraic in this case. This property of moraic segments which brings them on a par with the syllabic ones is stated in (10):[6]

(9) The set of moraic segments is a subset of the entire set of segments.

Thus both syllabic and moraic segments occupy a continuous portion of the sonority scale, including its sonorous end. It is then a language-specific property how far the syllabic, or the moraic, portion of the scale will extend towards the nonsonorous end. In other words, a universal property of languages is to have sets of moraic and syllabic segments; the memberships of these sets are then determined on a language-particular basis.

The question to be addressed at this point concerns the mutual relation between these two subsets of the segment inventory — that is, between the syllabic and the moraic segments. Note that the set of English moraic segments (8) properly includes the set of syllabic segments (7); as I argue here, the subset relation is what generally holds between these two sets:

(10) The set of syllabic segments is a subset of the set of moraic segments.

In other words, while both moraic and syllabic segments are always a subset of the segment inventory, syllabic segments are, in addition, a subset of moraic segments, as expressed explicitly in (11) (where Syl = the set of syllabic segments, Mor = the set of moraic segments, Seg = the entire set of segments):

(11) $\text{Syl} \subseteq \text{Mor} \subseteq \text{Seg}$

Note that (11) makes clear predictions: it sets the direction in which implicational relations should hold between different subsets of the segment inventory. In particular, one prediction is that the set of moraic segments can never be a proper subset of the set of syllabic segments:

(12) * $\text{Mor} \subset \text{Syl}$

Thus, the claim is that a language type characterized by (12) will belong to the class of impossible types.

Most importantly, the generalization in (11) also sets the range of *possible* language types. From (11) we obtain the following typology, with four logical possibilities:

(13) a. Type One: Syl ⊂ Mor = Seg
     b. Type Two: Syl = Mor ⊂ Seg
     c. Type Three: Syl ⊂ Mor ⊂ Seg
     d. Type Four: Syl = Mor = Seg

In what follows I argue that the typology in (13) makes correct predictions; that is, that it sets the range of all and only possible language types. Each of the four logical possibilities is reasonably well attested, as will be shown. In the next four sections I discuss each of the proposed types, pointing to a number of actual cases that illustrate them. Later in this chapter, I will discuss the hypothetical types such as (12), showing on what grounds they are to be excluded from the set of possible types.

Before turning to the discussion of each of the types, I will digress briefly to comment on the types of closed syllables that we should expect to find in each of the types. This issue will be discussed in more detail, and placed in a proper theoretical perspective, in section 2.8. Given the four language types in (13), we see that Type Two and Type Three contain segments which never contribute to weight, that is, which are nonmoraic; this is because in these language types the set of moraic segments is a proper subset of the segment inventory. The issue to be addressed here is whether nonmoraic segments can appear at the right syllable margin. As we will see, languages differ in this respect. Some, but not all, Type Two and Type Three languages will utilize the option of creating *light* closed syllables. First we may find the situation in which syllables closed with a moraic consonant have the structure in (14), and those closed with a nonmoraic consonant have the structure in (15); the former will be heavy, and the latter will be light (the representation here is due to Hyman 1985):

(14)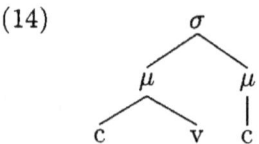

(15)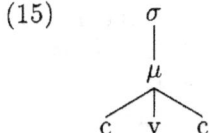

Second, while the structure in (14) will be generally available, the one in (15) will be left as a possible option for individual languages. Thus, adjoining an unmorified consonant to the preceding mora is an option that languages may but do not have to select.

2.3 Type One (Syl ⊂ Mor = Seg)

Of the proposed types, Type One, where the set of moraic segments is coextensive with the segment inventory, is the least controversial. Expressed in our terms, this means that any segment can head the second mora of a syllable and thus contribute to weight, which makes CVV as well as all CVC syllables heavy.

This type is represented by languages like Cairene Arabic (McCarthy 1979a), Aklan (Hayes 1981), and English; in all these cases syllable weight plays a crucial role in stress assignment, a phenomenon that is particularly sensitive to weight distinctions. Since this is a well attested type, it will not be necessary to present any details about the behavior of the languages that illustrate it. Rather, I turn at this point to those types whose existence is not as commonly assumed as is the case with this one.

In sum, all closed syllables in this language type are bimoraic, that is, have the structure as in (16):

(16)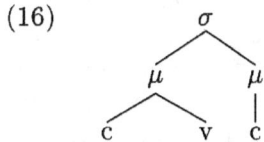

The open syllables will either be bimoraic, if they contain a long vowel, or monomoraic, if the vowel is short.

2.4 Type Two (Syl = Mor ⊂ Seg)

Type Two languages have been given a fair amount of attention in the literature, specifically in McCarthy 1979a, 1979b, Hayes 1981, 1982 and Levin 1985. Among the most common Type Two languages are those in which both the syllabic and the moraic sets contain only vowels; as a consequence, only CVV syllables are heavy, while CVC syllables are light. The most reliable diagnostic of this type of behavior has been provided again by stress systems. This behavior is associated, for example, with Khalkha Mongolian in which stress falls on the initial syllable if all syllables in the word contain a short vowel, otherwise on the leftmost syllable containing a long vowel or a diphthong (Street 1963). Although Khalkha Mongolian does have CVC syllables, they do not affect stress assignment, that is, they pattern with CV syllables. Thus, all Khalkha Mongolian syllables containing a short vowel are monomoraic, as shown in (17); this is equally true of open as well as of closed syllables.

(17) a.

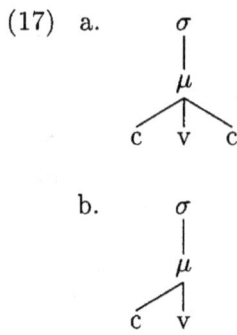

  b.

In contrast, the syllables with a long vowel are bimoraic, regardless of whether they are closed or not.

However, the situation we find in Khalkha Mongolian is not a necessary one for this language type. It is also conceivable to have a split into, say, moraic vowels and sonorants on the one hand, and nonmoraic obstruents on the other; the vowels and the sonorants would also be syllabic in this case. Although I am not aware of a language which behaves this way, the framework set here makes the prediction that such languages should not come as a surprise.

2.5 Type Three (Syl ⊂ Mor ⊂ Seg)

This is a controversial type, one that I will need to provide substantial arguments for. The characteristic trait of Type Three languages is that they divide up consonants into those that contribute to syllable weight and those that do not. Only the consonants of the former type will license the second mora of a bimoraic syllable:

(18)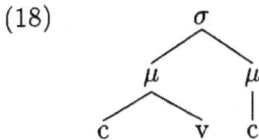

Nonmoraic consonants will be able to appear at the syllable margin in those languages which permit adjunction to the left. Thus, one possibility will be to find a language with two types of closed syllables, those that are light, as in (19), and those that are heavy, as in (18):

(19)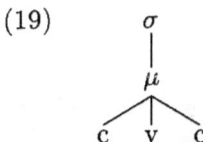

In this section we discuss four languages of this type. Danish, Lithuanian, and Kwakwala, discussed in subsections 2.5.1-2.5.3 allow two types of closed syllables, that is that they select the option of adjoining an unmorified consonant to the preceding mora, as discussed in section 2.2. The class of languages that do not select this option is illustrated here by Italian (subsection 2.5.4), which has only one type of closed syllable that occurs freely — those that are closed with a moraic consonant. Nonmoraic consonants may occur in the coda position only under some special strategy, for example as geminates, as is the case in Italian.[7]

2.5.1 Danish

One particular phenomenon in Danish – the so-called *stød* – can be accounted for in a natural way under the assumption that only some of the Danish consonants are moraic, which places Danish among Type Three languages. Stød is a mora-sensitive phenomenon, as observed by many, starting with Trubetzkoy 1969 (see also Liberman 1982, Clements and Keyser 1983).

According to Basbøll 1985, stød is a syllable prosody, manifested under the following set of conditions:[8]

(20) a. The syllable must bear stress (either primary or secondary).
b. The syllable must contain either a long vowel, or a short vowel immediately followed by a sonorant (including ð, which is a sonorant in Danish)

Examples of stød (marked by ') are given in (21):

(21) a. huu's   'house'
     b. lyy's   'light(adj.common)'
     c. lɔɔ's   'lock'
     d. soo'l   'son'
     e. hal'   'hall'
     f. man'   'man'
     g. ven'   'turn!'
     h. fʌl'g   'people'

One can generalize over these facts by saying that stød is associated with the second mora of a heavy syllable. This is appropriately illustrated by what Basbøll 1985:35 refers to as stylistic shortening; this rule is accompanied by a shift of stød from the vowel to the following consonant.[9]

(22) a. bɔɔ'ð vs. bɔð'   'boat'
     b. uu'ð vs. uð'   'out'
     c. boo'r vs. bor'   'table'

However, the situation is complicated by the failure of stød to appear on *all* closed syllables: only syllables containing a long vowel or a coda consonant of the right kind are traditionally described as having stød-basis, while all other syllables lack stød-basis.

I will adopt here the autosegmental analysis of stød proposed in Clements and Keyser 1983. Under their proposal stød is treated as an autosegment on the laryngeal tier which gets linked to the second mora of a syllable. However, since Clements and Keyser treat all closed syllables as bimoraic, the question arises how to assign stød to only a subset of consonants in the coda, or to only a subset of moras. To capture the fact that stød appears to be sensitive to segmental information, Clements and Keyser assign stød freely to all CVV and CVC syllables, regardless of whether they have stød-basis or not, and then delete it from syllables that do not have stød-basis. However, if Stød Linking is a lexical rule, this analysis would violate structure preservation; and, as shown in Basbøll 1985, there are good reasons to believe that stød is linked lexically, since it interacts with a number of morphological processes.

In the framework I am developing here, there is no need to assign stød to syllables that do not have stød-basis. In fact, it will be possible to say that syllables without stød basis do not meet the structural description of the linking rule. We can simply assume that only sonorants are in the set of moraic segments:

(23) Danish moraic segments:
ð
nasals
liquids
vowels

The rule of Stød Linking can then be formulated as in (24). Note that no segmental information is needed for its proper operation, since the second mora will be licensed by only those segments in the moraic set.

(24)   Stød Linking:

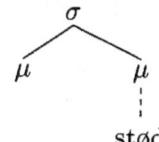

Syllables which have obstruents in the coda will have the structure in (25), and will therefore never meet the structural description for Stød Linking.[10]

(25)

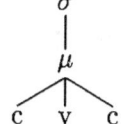

The analysis just sketched out is only meant to be suggestive of the situation to be found in a Type Three language. I am not aware of any additional data from Danish that would serve as supporting evidence for this particular analysis. We now turn to Lithuanian which depicts the situation characterized here in much more persuasive terms.

2.5.2 Lithuanian

In this subsection I will argue that Lithuanian should be analyzed as having moraic sonorants and nonmoraic obstruents (and no syllabic consonants). Only under this assumption can we account in a nonarbitrary fashion for an important difference between the lexical and postlexical phonological processes in Lithuanian. We will first look at the general properties of Lithuanian phonology, and then focus on the lexical and postlexical phonological processes respectively.

It has been observed a number of times, beginning with Trubetzkoy 1969, that the mora is a significant unit in the phonological system of Lithuanian. Moreover, the phonological phenomena that point to mora-sensitivity clearly show that Lithuanian moraic segments are not coextensive with the entire set of segments.

Mora-sensitivity is most perspicuous in the accentual system: Lithuanian is a pitch-accent language with three accents, each associated with certain tonal effects. The tone-bearing unit in Lithuanian is the mora, so that we find contour tones only on heavy syllables. One of the accent types, the circumflex accent, which has a rising melody, is represented by Kiparsky and Halle 1977 as a High tone on the second mora of a syllable. The circumflex accent can appear on syllables that contain a long vowel, or those closed with a sonorant. It cannot appear on syllables closed with an obstruent. (26) lists cases of words with the circumflex accent:

(26)   a.   CVV: vỹnas 'wine', peĩlis 'knife', zuĩkis 'rabbit'
        b.   CVL: gaŕsas 'sound', baĺsas 'voice'
        c.   CVN: šim̃tas 'hundred', lañkas 'rainbow'

Under a tonal analysis of the Lithuanian accent, we can represent the three Lithuanian accents as in (27):

(27) a. Acute (x́):

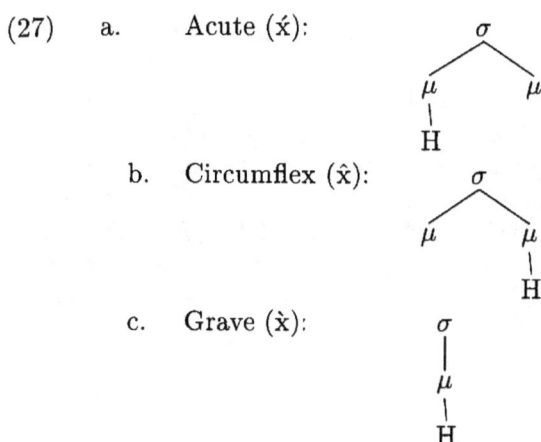

b. Circumflex (x̂):

c. Grave (x̀):

According to this representation, the circumflex accent (which we are focusing on here) corresponds to a High tone linked to the second mora of a syllable. Under this assumption, the pattern in (26) strongly suggests that obstruents are not moraic, that is, that the set of moraic segments in Lithuanian is that in (28):

(28) Lithuanian moraic segments:
nasals
liquids
vowels

This is independently supported by the so-called leftward accent retraction, described in Senn 1966:51. According to Senn, accent retracts from a final syllable if it has a grave or a circumflex accent, as in (29) and (30), but not if its accent is acute, as in 31.

(29) a. šakà vs. šàka
b. giivà vs. giĩva

(30) a. laukaĩ vs. laũkai
b. arkliũ vs. arĩkliu

(31) gerám vs. gerám

This brings together the grave and the circumflex accent, which both have tone linked to the final mora, as distinct from the acute accent which does not. A plausible restatement of accent retraction in terms of the representation of the accents in (27) is as follows: tone retracts if it is linked to the final mora of a final syllable.

Although Senn does not illustrate a full range of cases, some of the cases are well documented. As shown in the examples below, tone retracts from a final short syllable, as in (32)a, from the second mora of a long syllable, as in (32)c, or from a syllable closed with an obstruent, as in (32)b, but not from a syllable closed with a sonorant, as in (32)d.

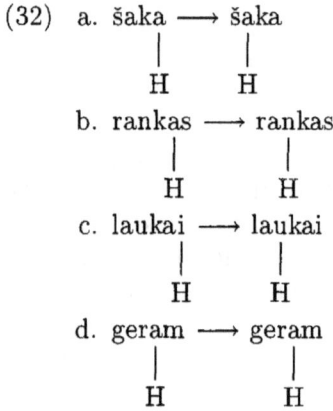

We can account for this pattern by saying that the High tone shifts from the last mora in a word; it is indeed linked to the last mora in (32)a, b, and c, but not in (32)d, where the last mora is the sonorant m. Thus s in (32)b is not moraic but m in (32)d is. Moreover, these facts match with those about the distribution of the circumflex accent; in both cases obstruents behave like segments that are not heading a mora. In sum, the two sets of facts discussed here receive a natural explanation only under the assumption that (28) lists all and only moraic segments in Lithuanian.

It can be shown in fact that the distinction between moraic sonorants and nonmoraic obstruents pervades the entire Lithuanian phonological system. Lithuanian obeys the so-called Osthoff's Law, which Kenstowicz 1971 formulates as in (33):

(33)   V ⟶ ∅ / V ___ [l,r,m,n] C

Sonority Constraints on Moras

According to (33), long vowels become short when followed by a tautosyllabic sonorant. An important consequence of this is that the types of syllables available throughout the lexical component are those in (34) (where S stands for sonorant, and C for any consonant):

(34) a. CV, CVV
 b. CVO, CVVO
 c. CVS, *CVVS

That is to say, open syllables and syllables closed with an obstruent can contain either a long or a short vowel, while syllables closed with a sonorant can only have a short vowel. If sonorants are moraic and obstruents are not, then we can view the inventory in (34) as resulting from the following constraint:

(35) A syllable may have at most two moras.

In other words, Lithuanian prohibits superheavy syllables. Both CVV and CVVO syllables are bimoraic, and therefore conform to Constraint (35); but because sonorants are moraic, CVVS syllables are superheavy, and therefore prohibited by this constraint.

But what is the domain of (35)? In what follows I show that this constraint is operative only in the lexical component, that is, in the subpart of the grammar characterized by structure preservation. Lithuanian does have superheavy syllables on the surface; but as I will argue, they arise only as a result of certain lengthening processes that apply postlexically, i.e., in the component of the grammar where structure preservation no longer holds.

In order to show how Constraint (35) operates in the grammar of Lithuanian, we will examine several phonological processes, all pertaining to the vocalic system. In my analysis, I closely follow Kenstowicz 1971 and the arguments advanced therein for the various inventories of the vocalic segments in the language.

According to Kenstowicz 1971, the surface vowel inventory in Lithuanian is as in (36):[11]

(36) i: i u: u
 e: o:
 e̞: e̞ a: a

The system contains two sets of long nonhigh vowels, distinguished only by tenseness: e: and o: are tense, and ẹ: and ạ: are lax. The short nonhigh vowels are both lax.

Next, Kenstowicz shows that the tense vowels e: and o: alternate on a regular basis with the short lax vowels e and a. Furthermore, the long lax vowels ẹ: and ạ: participate in alternations that arise at a much later point, and are not part of the 'initial' inventory. From this, it follows that the underlying vowel inventory in Lithuanian is as in (37):

(37) i: i   u: u
      e: e   o: a

Building upon this, I will further assume that the system in (37) is present throughout the lexical component; and that, due to structure preservation, it captures all lexical contrasts. The system in (36), on the other hand, arises only postlexically.

As already observed, Constraint (35) is operative only in the lexical component. But if it places restrictions on the vocalic alternations solely in this component, then it should operate within the range of the system in (37). In other words, the vowel system that arises postlexically, that is, the system in (36), should be outside the domain of Constraint (35), and this is exactly what we find. It is the system in (36), rather than the one in (37), that gives rise to superheavy syllables, in violation of Constraint (35).

2.5.2.1 Lexical Component

I focus here on two lexical processes whose effect can roughly be characterized as mora addition — Ablaut and Nasal Infixation. Neither of these processes can create superheavy syllables, in keeping with Constraint (35), which confirms my claim that this constraint is operative in the lexical component. In what follows I show how these two processes interact with the constraint on syllable weight. I will first discuss Ablaut, and then Nasal Infixation.

Ablaut is a morphologically governed process whose effect is to lengthen the vowel of the root. I argued above that, within the lexicon, short lax vowels regularly alternate with tense vowels; that is, that the range of lexical alternations is determined by the system in (37) above. This is certainly true of Ablaut, which creates the following contrasts:

(38) a. i ⟶ i:
     b. u ⟶ u:
     c. e ⟶ e:
     d. a ⟶ o:

Ablaut can be formulated as adding a 'new' nonhead mora to the affected syllable, as in (39):

(39)   Ablaut:

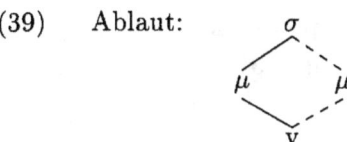

The newly added mora will be linked to the closest tautosyllabic vowel by a process reminiscent of compensatory lengthening. Since this process will apply as soon as the new mora becomes available, it will apply in the lexicon, and therefore create the contrasts listed in (38).

We will now see how this process applies to different kinds of verbal roots. Following Kenstowicz, I divide ablauting roots into three classes, listed in (40):

(40) a. roots with a short vowel followed by an obstruent (*tup-* 'perch', *vag-* 'steal', *dreb-* 'splash')
     b. roots with a short vowel followed by a sonorant (*kar* 'hang', *vir* 'boil', *mir* 'die')
     c. roots with a diphthong (*kau-* 'beat')

As already mentioned, Ablaut is a morphologically conditioned rule. It is associated with the verbal system, and applies in the infinitive and the preterite, but not in the present form. However, no effect of Ablaut is evidenced in the infinitive forms of (40)b,c types of roots. This will be attributed to the interference of Constraint 35, as I show in a moment.

We will first inspect the roots of type (40)a. As shown in (41) – (43), Ablaut applies freely to roots of this type, never conflicting with Constraint (35).

(41)   Present   Preterite   Infinitive
            tup]ia   tup]ee   tup]ti
   Ablaut   —   tuup]ee   tuup]ti

(42)   Present   Preterite   Infinitive
            vag]ia   vag]ee   vag]ti
   Ablaut   —   voog]ee   voog]ti

(43)   Present   Preterite   Infinitive
            dreb]ia   dreb]ee   dreb]ti
   Ablaut   —   dreeb]ee   dreeb]ti

But the situation is much less straightforward with roots of the 40b. type, i.e., those that have a short vowel followed by a sonorant. Here we will see a difference between the preterite and the infinitive forms; the effect of Ablaut is manifested in the former but not in the latter case. This difference is traditionally attributed to Osthoff's Law: long vowels become short when followed by a tautosyllabic sonorant. In our terms, this is due to Constraint 35, which prohibits the occurrence of trimoraic syllables.

Let us now look at the derivations of the forms that contain sonorants in the root. In particular, I will claim that although Ablaut may add another mora, this mora will remain unlinked, since its linking to the syllable node would violate Constraint (35). Being unlinked, this mora eventually undergoes stray erasure.

(44)   Present   Preterite   Infinitive
            kar]ia   kar]ee   kar]ti
   Ablaut   —   koor]ee   koor]ti
   Output   karia   kooree   kar]ti

(45)   Present   Preterite   Infinitive
            vir]ia   vir]ee   vir]ti
   Ablaut   —   viir]ee   viir]ti
   Output   viria   viiree   vir]ti

(46) 	 Present Preterite Infinitive
        	 mir]ia mir]ee mir]ti
    Ablaut 	— miir]ee miir]ti
    Output 	miria miiree mir]ti

Note that the effect of Ablaut is 'neutralized' precisely in those cases where it produces a trimoraic syllable, which supports the present view that 'shortening' applies only when Ablaut creates a superheavy syllable.

Finally, let us look at the behavior of forms which contain a diphthong, i.e., those in (40)c. Here Ablaut also creates superheavy syllables in the infinitive; and again, the 'shortening' rescues those forms whose syllable structure violates Constraint (35).

(47) 	 Present Preterite Infinitive
        	 kau]ia kau]ee kau]ti
    Ablaut 	— koou]ee koou]ti
    Output 	kauja koovee kau]ti

Note that the present analysis places the burden of explanation solely on Constraint (35). This constraint is independently needed to prevent the creation of superheavy syllables which do not result from the application of Ablaut. Kenstowicz 1970:83 mentions two such cases, listed in (48):

(48) a. puolee *vs.* pulti 'tumble'
     b. aštuoni 'eight' *vs.* aštuntas 'eighth'

Clearly, in these cases we have to posit a diphthong underlyingly; this diphthong is then reduced to a monophthong precisely when it ends up in a syllable closed with a sonorant, by virtue of Constraint (35).

Ablaut thus shows that CVVO syllables behave as bimoraic, while CVVS syllables are trimoraic, and therefore prohibited by Constraint (35). In sum, we see that the constraint on superheavy syllables is fully operative in the subpart of phonology in which Ablaut applies.

Nasal infixes are introduced by a complex morphological process: a class of derived intransitives (mostly inchoatives) are formed by two distinct morphological mechanisms — by 'infixing' a nasal, and by adding the suffix -*st*. In certain cases we find that these two processes apply jointly, while in others only one applies to the exclusion of the other. I do not address this particular problem here, since my focus will be on nasal infixes and their effect on syllable weight.

The relevance of nasal infixes in the present context is that they increase the number of moras in the root final syllable, and thus potentially interact with Constraint (35). Again we will find a crucial difference between roots whose final syllable has an obstruent in the coda and those with a sonorant in this position. In the latter case we will encounter violations of the prohibition on superheavy syllables.

The nasal infix will be represented as a nasal segment (unspecified for place) which is linked to a mora, as shown in (49):[12]

(49) μ
$\quad\;|$
$\quad\;\text{N}$

For reasons to be given in a moment, we will need a yet finer classification of roots than was necessary for Ablaut. That is, we need to separate out roots whose final syllable is closed with a stop, those whose final syllable is closed with a fricative, and those that end in a sonorant. We will look at these in the given order.

If the root syllable is closed with a stop, we find the insertion of a nasal infix, but suffixation does not apply:

(50)
	ak	šlap	ged
Nasal Infix	aNk	šlaNp	geNd
Suffixation	—	—	—
'Shortening'	—	—	—
Other Rules	aŋka	šlampa	genda
Output	aŋka	šlampa	genda

Nasal Infixation interacts with several other processes of a fairly general nature, all involving nasal consonants. When a nasal is followed by a stop, it undergoes assimilation in place, as shown under 'Other Rules' in (50). These processes, as well as the others that affect nasals, belong to the postlexical component, and I mention them here only in passing.

When they precede consonants other than stops, nasals undergo elision. Thus, in syllables closed with a fricative, nasal infixes do not appear on the surface. Note that with these roots we find suffixation as well as the insertion of nasal infixes.

(51)
	gris	miš	šaš
Nasal Infix	griNs	miNš	šaNš
Suffixation	griNs]st	miNš]st	šaNš]st
Other Rules	griNs]t	miNš]t	šaNš]t
Inflection	griNst]a	miNšt]a	šaNšt]a
Other Rules	griista	miišta	šaašta
Output	griista	miišta	šaašta

That the nasal infix is indeed 'there' can be shown by compensatory lengthening which links a vocalic segment to the mora vacated by nasal elision.[13] Thus although the root has a short vowel, the vowel in the output form is long, which will be taken as evidence that adding a nasal infix to a syllable results in an increase of its weight.

Now that we have established that nasal infixes affect syllable weight, we will look at the crucial case — that of roots which end in a sonorant. Note that the addition of the suffix -*st* is optional in this case. And, it is important to bear in mind that the nasals are deleted before a sonorant as well.

(52)
	bal	bal
Nasal Infix	baNl	baNl
Suffixation	—	baNl]st
'Shortening'	—	bal]st
Inflection	baNl]a	balst]a
Other Rules	baala	—
Output	baala	balsta

Here, we see an important difference between the suffixed form and the form with no suffix added. If the suffix is there, the nasal infix can only syllabify to the left, as a 'coda' consonant. However, since its linking to the syllable node would create a superheavy syllable, in violation of Constraint (35), the nasal infix fails to be linked and is lost by stray erasure. In the unsuffixed form, the final sonorant is in the onset of the following syllable, so that the nasal infix ends up linked to the syllable node, creating a heavy, but not a superheavy, syllable. Thus, the output form has a long vowel, which results from compensatory lengthening triggered by nasal elision.

In sum, nasal infixes interact with the constraint on syllable weight. They are incorporated into syllable structure only if the resulting syllable conforms to Constraint (35), otherwise they are lost due to stray erasure.

2.5.2.2 Postlexical Component

The postlexical rule we will examine here departs from structure preservation in at least two respects — by increasing the vowel inventory from (37) to (36), and by bypassing the constraint on syllable weight.

The rule in question, which Halle and Kiparsky 1981 refer to as Nonfinal Lengthening, lengthens accented, nonfinal a and e, creating the following contrasts (taken from Kenstowicz 1971:4):

(53) a. leẽdas 'ice-nom.sg.' vs. ledè 'ice-loc.sg.'
      b. kaãsa 'dig-3sg.pres.' vs. kasù 'dig-1sg.pres.'

This rule violates structure preservation in two ways. First, it creates long lax vowels, as in (53), where both a: in $ka{:}sa$ and e: in $le{:}das$ are lax. Second, this rule creates superheavy syllables, as shown in (54):

(54) a. láangas 'window-nom.sg.' vs. langẽ 'window-loc.sg.'
      b. béernas 'servant-nom.sg.' vs. bernaĩ 'servant-nom.pl.'

These two facts strongly suggest that the Rule of Nonfinal Lengthening applies postlexically. Also, it shows that Constraint 35 does not operate in the postlexical component. Thus, postlexically we do find superheavy syllables, but strictly within the postlexical range of vowel contrasts.

2.5.3 Kwakwala

Kwakwala is of particular interest in the present context because its closed syllables clearly fall into two classes — those that are light and those that are heavy. Evidence for this comes from several phonological processes, one of them being the assignment of stress.

In his descriptive study of Kwakwala, Boas 1947 comments on the special status of certain consonants — specifically m, n, l, y and w — in the phonological system of the language. According to Boas, of particular interest is the fact that a sequence consisting of a vowel and any of the consonants just listed

> ... has to be considered as a long vowel, except only in those cases in which the stem ... is followed by a suffix with initial vowel that does not induce any modification of the stem. [Boas 1947:209]

Boas illustrates this by one particular type of reduplication, which affects stems whose initial syllable contains either a long vowel or a vowel followed by a sonorant. Reduplication is triggered by various morphological processes; we will look here at cases of reduplication triggered by a set of suffixes. One such suffix is -m'ut/-mut, which has two allophones: -m'ut (with a glottalized nasal) comes after stems that end either in a voiced or in a glottalized stop, and -mut is used in all other environments.

When mut is added to a root with a long vowel, the reduplication pattern is as in (55):[14]

(55) a. qá:-qas-mut 'tracks' (root qa:s) (p. 340)
   b. x^{w}á:-x^{w}aƛ-m'ut 'remains of fish cutting' (root x^{w}a:ƛ-) (p.209)
   c. c'á:-c'əs-m'ut 'old eel-grass' (root c'a:s)

Note that the root vowel is shortened, while the reduplicated syllable preserves the original vowel length. The same basic pattern is found with roots that contain a vowel plus sonorant sequence: both the vowel and the sonorant appear in the reduplicated syllable, which brings out the analogy with long vowels that Boas observed. Furthermore, the root syllable is again 'shortened', only this time the shortening is realized as loss of the sonorant. This is illustrated in (56):

(56) a. m'ál-m'ə-d^{z}o 'white on surface' (root m'əl-) (p.209)
   b. sál-sə-m'ut 'what is left after drilling' (root səl-) (p.209)
   c. yán-yat-m'ut 'gnawing of a large animal' (root yənt-) (p.209)

By contrast, if the root contains an obstruent following the vowel plus sonorant sequence, this other consonant is not reduplicated, nor is it 'deleted' from the root as part of the shortening process:

(57) a. qə́n-qas-mut 'chips' (root qəns) (p.340)
   b. xə́l-xat-m'ut 'sawdust' (root xəlt (p.340)

Because of this peculiar behavior of sonorants, Boas occasionally refers to them as 'syllabic consonants'. Yet sonorants are not syllabic consonants in the common sense of this term, since they never occupy the nuclear position in any of the surface syllables. But the special status of sonorants becomes much less mysterious after we have examined the status of sonorants in Danish. We can simply assume that in Kwakwala only sonorants belong to the set of moraic segments:

(58) Kwakwala moraic segments (first approximation):
   nasals
   liquids
   vowels

Thus, what makes the vowel plus sonorant sequence similar to a long vowel is that both are bimoraic, as distinct from a vowel plus obstruent sequence which is monomoraic.

Since both vowels and sonorants are moraic, it follows that CVV and CVS syllables will pattern together. But this further suggests that we should also find cases in which CVO syllables pattern with CV syllables in that both are light. In fact, this distinction is essential for the Kwakwala stress system, which is of the quantity-sensitive type: CVS and CVV syllables are treated by the stress rules as heavy, and CV and CVO syllables are treated as light.

That Kwakwala is indeed a quantity-sensitive stress language can be seen by inspecting how syllables with long vowels affect the distribution of stress. The examples below show that stress falls on the leftmost syllable containing a long vowel, as in (59), and on the last one if no syllable contains a long vowel, as in (60).[15]

(59) a. qá:sa 'to walk' (p.218)
   b. n'a:la 'day' (p.218)
   c. c'é:k^{w}a 'bird' (p.218)
   d. x^{w}á:k^w'əna 'canoe' (p.246)
   e. x^{w}á:x^{w}ək^w'əna 'canoe (pl)' (p.246)

f. t'əli:dᶻu   'large board on which fish are cut' (Grubb, p.207)

(60) a. nəpá   'to throw a round thing' (p.218)
    b. bəxá   'to cut' (p.218)
    c. w'ədá   'it is cold' (p.218)
    d. x̱ək'á   'to stay away' (p.218)
    e. m'əkʷəlá   'moon' (p.218)
    f. c'əxəlá   'to be sick' (p.218)
    g. gətəx̱ʷá   'to tickle' (p.217)
    h. məc'ətá (pl.)   'to heal' (p.248)

The words in (59)–(60) contain only open syllables. This clearly establishes the fact that CVV syllables are wheavy and CV syllables are light. If we add to this inventory the CVO syllables, we see that they pattern with the CV rather than with the CVV type, since they never obtain stress:

(61) a. c'ətxá   'to squirt' (p.218)
    b. təƛc'á   'to warm oneself' (p.217)
    c. səxʷc'á   'to be willing' (p.217)
    d. kʷ'əsxá   'to splash' (p.217)
    e. maxʷc'á   'to be ashamed' (p.217)
    f. gasxá   'to carry on fingers' (p.217)

However, a syllable closed with a sonorant patterns with the CVV type, i.e., a vowel plus sonorant sequence "has to be considered as a long vowel," as Boas put it.

(62) a. m'ə́nsa   'to measure' (p. 218)
    b. də́lxa   'damp' (p. 218)
    c. tə́lqʷa   'soft' (p. 218)
    d. mə́ndᶻa   'to make kindling food' (p. 218)
    e. dᶻə́mbətəls   'to bury in hole in ground' (p.218)
    f. məxə́nx̱ənd   'to strike edge' (p.219)

Within the typology proposed in Hayes 1981, 1993 and Prince 1985, this stress pattern is classified as belonging to the unbounded type, with foot structure assigned as follows (after Hayes 1993):

(63) a. *Foot Construction:* Parse a word into right-headed quantity-sensitive, unbounded feet.
b. *Word Layer Construction:* End Rule Left.

The following derivations demonstrate how stress is assigned in accordance with (63):

(64) (x)   (x)   (x)   (x)
      (x)   (x)   (x)   (. x)
      qá:sa   c'é:k^{w}a   x^{w}á:x^{w}ək^w'əna   t'əlí:d^{z}u

      (x)   (x)   (x)   (x)
      (. x)   (. . x)   (. x)   (. x)
      nəpá   m'ək^{w}əlá   c'ətxá   təƛc'á

      (x)   (x)   (x)   (x)
      (x)   (x)   (x) (. x)   (. x) (x)
      m'ə́nsa   də́lxa   d^{z}ə́mbətəls   məxə́nx̣ənd

But the situation in Kwakwala is still more complex. Kwakwala has a rich inventory of consonants, in part because voiceless obstruents and sonorants come in two series – glottalized and unglottalized. This is shown in the consonant chart below, adapted from Boas 1947.[16] (Consonants belonging to the glottalized series are marked with a ' sign.)

(65) Kwakwala consonants

p	t	c	ƛ	k	k^w	q	q^w	
b	d	d^z	λ	g	g^w	g̣	g̣^{w}	ʔ
p'	t'	c'	ƛ'	k'	k^w'	q'	q^w'	
		s	l	x	x^w	x̣	x̣^{w}	h
m'	n'		l'	w'	y'			
m	n		l	w	y			

Thus, sonorants can be either glottalized or unglottalized, and it is only in this latter case that they are also moraic. In view of this, we propose a revised inventory of Kwakwala moraic segments:

(66) Kwakwala moraic segments:
(unglottalized) nasals
(unglottalized) liquids
vowels

Thus glottalized sonorants are not moraic, and in this respect they behave like obstruents. This is illustrated in (67), where stress rules treat syllables closed with glottalized sonorants as light:

(67) a. gəm'x̣á 'to use the left hand' (p.219)
   b. k{ʷ}ən'x̣á 'clams are spoiled' (p.219)
   c. məl'qá 'to repair canoe' (p.219)

Boas (p.219) lists the following minimal pairs, one containing a glottalized and the other a nonglottalized sonorant. As expected, this difference is accompanied by different positions of stress:

(68) a. an'qá 'to put fire among' vs. ánqa 'to squeeze'
   b. gəl'qá 'to wipe the anus' vs. gə́lqa 'to swim'
   c. gəm'x̣á 'to use the left hand' vs. gə́mx̣a 'carrying wood in arms' (Grubb, p.172)

Furthermore, certain suffixes cause the glottalization of stem-final consonants. If the stem-final consonant is a sonorant, we also find change in the position of stress, as shown below (Boas 1947:218). Thus, the suffix in (69)a causes the glottalization of the preceding sonorant (following Boas' conventions, this is shown by the = mark), while the suffix in (69)b is neutral:

(69) a. gəl'=d^{z}ó:d 'to crawl on flat thing'
   b. gələ́– c'o:d 'to crawl in a thing'

Bach 1978 classifies glottalized sonorants among obstruents, to account for their obstruent-like behavior. Note that this kind of move is not necessary under our assumptions. It might be the case that phonetically, glottalized sonorants have the properties of obstruents. But if this is not so, we still have the option of saying that glottalized segments are less sonorous than nonglottalized segments, and that this is equally true of sonorants and of obstruents. Thus, moraic segments can correspond to only a subset of sonorants, just as they can correspond to only a subset of consonants.

To sum up, the facts about stress assignment in Kwakwala present a particularly strong argument for the present approach. Stress rules are among the least likely to be sensitive to segmental information. In particular, it would be quite odd to assume that all CVC syllables are heavy, and then to constrain foot construction, as well as other relevant processes, on the basis of detailed information about melodic structure. But if we assume that only a subset of consonants are moraic, Kwakwala stress system turns out to be quite simple, as well as compatible with the proposed typologies.

2.5.4 Italian

According to Itô 1986, a number of languages block the occurrence of certain segments in the coda. In Italian, for example, only sonorants and *s* are allowed in the coda while obstruents (with the exception of *s*) are prohibited in this position.[17] The lists in (70) and (71) are taken from Itô 1986:

(70) in.flessibile 'inflexible'
      al.tro 'other'
      bur.gravio 'castle lord'
      em.blema 'emblem'
      es.presso 'express'

(71) *it.flessibile
      ap.tro
      bud.gravio
      eg.blema
      ec.presso

The triconsonantal clusters in the above examples consist of a coda consonant followed by two onset consonants, since the maximum syllable in Italian is, according to Itô (and the references therein), of the CCVC type.

Itô proposes to handle these facts by positing coda conditions, in the form of negative constraints. Thus, the Coda Condition for Italian has the following form:

(72) Italian Coda Condition: *Coda
 |
 [− son]

The purpose of this mechanism is to prohibit the occurrence of a certain class of segments under one of the subsyllabic nodes. However, one property of this constraint systematically recurs in constraints proposed by Itô for other languages (for example, Japanese): segments whose occurrence is prohibited belong to the class of obstruents, that is, to the class of nonsonorous consonants. But this does not follow from anything in Itô's proposal. In particular, nothing will prevent us from positing constraints like the following:

(73) *Coda
 |
 [+son]

Yet, restrictions like these are not found, although Itô's system allows them in principle.

I will now show that positing sets of moraic and syllabic segments is an alternative to the kinds of constraints that Itô proposes. Furthermore, this is a more desirable solution since, in addition to restricting the set of segments that can appear in the coda, we further predict in which direction sonority will be restricted. We can simply propose that the set of Italian moraic segments is as in (74):

(74) Italian moraic segments:
 s
 nasals
 liquids
 vowels

It follows then that only the segments in (74) will be allowed to appear under the second mora of the syllable. Furthermore, these are the only segments that can appear at the right margin of the syllable: unlike Danish, Lithuanian, and Kwakwala, Italian does not allow adjunction of a nonmoraic segment at the right syllable margin. Thus, since obstruents are not moraic, they are excluded from this position. And, of course, we cannot have the case of a language which has moraic obstruents but nonmoraic sonorants, which explains why constraints like (73) are to be excluded from the grammar.

However, *geminate* obstruents are allowed in the coda; in order to account for these cases Itô appeals to geminate inalterability, and I adopt here the essence of her solution. We could say that languages which do not allow adjunction of nonmoraic segments at the right syllable margin adhere to a filter which blocks nonmoraic segments in this position. If we assume that the filter contains a single link, geminates will be able to evade its effect due to their special linking status.

2.6 Type Four (Syl = Mor = Seg)

Like Type Three, Type Four is also controversial, but for a different reason: this type assumes the existence of syllabic obstruents, an assumption which is difficult to reconcile with the the commonly held belief that syllabicity correlates with a certain minimal degree of sonority. However, several cases have been reported in the literature which question this belief. According to Hoard 1978, a number of Pacific Northwest Indian languages do have syllabic obstruents. And Imdlawn Tashlhiyt Berber, which we will inspect here in detail, clearly demonstrates that Type Four is within the range of attestable types.

2.6.1 Imdlawn Tashlhiyt Berber

In the discussion of Imdlawn Tashlhiyt Berber (henceforth ITB), I follow the analysis in Dell and Elmedlaoui 1985. A striking property of this dialect of Berber is that any of its segments can be syllabic, including even those at the nonsonorous end of the scale. Thus, ITB depicts precisely the situation predicted by Type Four of our typology: in this language, the sets of syllabic and moraic segments are coextensive with the segment inventory. The most obvious question that comes to mind is how obstruents function under such circumstances. As evidenced by the following examples, all obstruents including even voiceless stops, can form syllable peaks (syllabic consonants are capitalized):

(75) a. tS.ti 'she selected'
 b. u.tXk 'I struck you'
 c. tF.tKt 'you suffered a sprain'

Below are given further examples, whose purpose is to show that whether a consonant is syllabic or not is largely determined by the context. (76) lists second person perfective forms (the second person marker is *t-* ... *-t*), each containing two syllabic consonants:

(76) a. tRgLt 'lock'
b. tSkRt 'do'
c. tXzNt 'store'
d. tZdMt 'gather wood'
e. tLbŽt 'step onto'
f. tRkSt 'hide'
g. tNšFt 'graze (skin)"
h. tMsXt 'transform'

However, with a different suffix added (in this case *-as*), the forms in (77) have a single syllabic consonant:

(77) a. tRglas 'lock'
b. tSkras 'do'
c. tXznas 'store'
d. tZdmas 'gather wood'
e. tLbžas 'idem'
f. tRksas 'hide'
g. tNšfas 'graze (skin)'
h. tMsxas 'transform'

Thus, the syllabicity of consonants in ITB is predictable from their sonority; for a consonant to be syllabic, it has to be followed (as well as preceded) by a less or equally sonorous segment. This kind of behavior has been observed on a smaller scale in other languages with syllabic consonants or high vowel/glide alternations but, as observed in Dell and Elmedlaoui, it is a central feature of syllabification in ITB. The reason for this is that in ITB all segments can potentially occupy the nuclear position in the syllable.

One has to wonder about the phonetic rendering of sequences like *tF.tKt* or *tZ.dMt*. The authors note that in some, although not in all cases, an ultrashort transitional vowel is inserted to ease the pronunciation of consonant sequences. Interestingly though, such vowels are inserted only between voiced consonants; voiceless consonants are produced without intervening vocalic transitions.

Moreover, Dell and Elmedlaoui offer a further argument that the ITB syllabic consonants indeed function as syllable peaks. The evidence comes from the so-called emphatic articulation which stretches over a sequence of segments, respecting syllable structure. This is of particular interest in cases where the emphatic articulation crosses word boundaries, obviously following the pattern of syllabification across words. An example of this is given in (78), where the last consonant of a word is adjoined to the following, word-initial vowel (emphatic articulation is marked by dots underneath segments):

(78) yazd isdu 'he came near and leaned (on something)'

Note that the *s* in the coda of the syllable *dis* is not affected by this process, which does not go beyond the nucleus; or in our terms, beyond the mora boundary. But observe the following:

(79) yiwititt Ṣdarun 'he feels like going to your place'

Here, the initial *s* in *Sdarun* is affected by emphatic pronunciation because it is a syllable nucleus. Note that if the initial segment of a word is not a syllable nucleus, as is the case with *dumn* in (80), it will not be affected by emphatic pronunciation.

(80) ha sdis dumn 'here are six that last'

The pattern in (78)–(80) argues persuasively that the nuclear function is associated with the syllabic consonant until a relatively late point in the derivation, that is, beyond the lexical component.

2.7 Sonority of Moras and Sonority of Syllables

As shown in sections 2.3.–2.6, all language types predicted by the typology proposed in section 2.2. are indeed possible and attested types. The typology is repeated in (81), supplied with a list of languages that illustrate individual types:

(81) a. Type One: Syl ⊂ Mor = Seg
       (Cairene Arabic, English, Aklan)
    b. Type Two: Syl = Mor ⊂ Seg
       (Khalkha Mongolian)
    c. Type Three: Syl ⊂ Mor ⊂ Seg
       (Danish, Kwakwala)
    d. Type Four: Syl = Mor = Seg
       (Imdlawn Tashlhiyt Berber, Northwest Indian Languages)

Let us now turn to the impossible types, and see on what grounds they are to be excluded. Recall the basic implicational relation which served as source for all the generalizations proposed here:

(82) Syl ⊆ Mor ⊆ Seg

Note that (82) excludes the following as impossible types:

(83) * Seg ⊂ Mor

(84) * Seg ⊂ Syl

(85) * Mor ⊂ Syl

Of course, the entire set of segments cannot be a proper subset of any of the special subsets, which naturally excludes (83) and (84). More importantly, it also follows that the set of moraic segments cannot be a proper subset of the set of syllabic segments. In what follows, I will show that this latter statement need not be stipulated; rather it can be derived from the framework I am developing here. With only one addition, that of subsyllabic metrical structure, the claim about the subset relation between the sets of syllabic and moraic segments follows directly from the representation itself.

We will begin by taking a closer look at the asymmetries between the two moras of a heavy syllable. Recall that, although sonority requirements are placed on every single mora, they may vary with the position of that mora within syllable structure. These are precisely the facts we cover by attaching the labels 'syllabic' and 'moraic' to segments which head moras. But what is the source of these asymmetries?

Following Kiparsky 1979, 1981, I will assume that syllables have subsyllabic metrical structure. Kiparsky proposes to represent the syllable as in (86), that is, in the form of a metrical tree:

(86)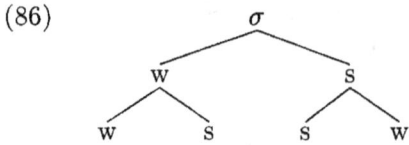

What is gained by this kind of representation is that degrees of sonority within the syllable are encoded as degrees of prominence. As in any other metrical tree, the most prominent portion of the syllable is linked to the root node by an uninterrupted sequence of s nodes. It thus follows as a necessary consequence of this representation that the syllable contains at most one prominence peak.

However, this representation is insufficiently constrained. It places no limit on the number of subsyllabic constituents; and as noted in Clements and Keyser 1983:7-8, it assigns different structure to heavy syllables of different length. But if the labeling device proposed by Kiparsky is incorporated into a structure parsed into subsyllabic constituents, we can salvage the advantages of this proposal. In particular, this specific device for characterizing prominence can be incorporated into the representation we have been utilizing here:

(87)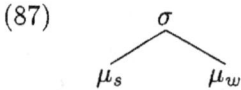

This move is very much in the vein of Selkirk 1980, where (suprasyllabic) metrical structure of the arboreal type (as in Liberman and Prince 1977) is recast in terms of a new type of prosodic constituent — the foot. Selkirk retains the s w labeling, but this time labels are placed on primitive prosodic constituents rather than on the nodes of the metrical tree. Mine is precisely the same move, only in a different domain. I have replaced the arboreal metrical structure at the subsyllabic level by prosodic constituents, again retaining the *s w* labeling as an encoder of relative prominence.

Although the representation in (87) involves a less hierarchical structure than that in (86), one similarity clearly remains: the most sonorous part of the syllable is linked to the root by an *s*-labeled mora. We can further assume that the leftmost mora, the one carrying the *s* label, is the head of the syllable. The sonority requirements of the syllable are then passed down the *s* path and inherited by the mora occupying this position.

Most importantly, with the representation in (87) we derive the subset relation between the sets of syllabic and moraic segments. Note that the segment in *s* position needs to be sufficiently sonorous to head *both* the mora *and* the syllable. If so, then the sonority requirements on syllables cannot go beyond those imposed on moras. To illustrate this, observe what would happen in a hypothetical (but impossible) case of a language with the following sets of syllabic and moraic segments:

(88) X's syllabic segments:
vowels
liquids
nasals

(89) X's moraic segments:
vowels
liquids

Note that in our hypothetical case nasals are syllabic but not moraic. This would give rise to a conflict if a nasal appeared under the strong (that is, *s*-labeled) mora. In particular, a nasal would be licensed by the sonority conditions on syllables, but prohibited by the sonority conditions on moras. Thus, although the memberships of the two sets are in principle independent of each other, the representation imposes constraints which ensure that the syllabic segments be a subset of the moraic ones.

More generally, in order to satisfy the sonority requirements both of moras and of syllables, the segment that heads the *s* mora has to belong to the intersection of these two sets, and this is what forces a subset relation on the sets of syllabic and moraic segments. Of course, it is the sonority requirements of the *syllable* rather than those of the mora that will win over, since the intersection includes all (and only) syllabic segments.

Note that no constraints of this sort are placed on the rightmost mora, which obtains the w label. The sonority of this mora is controlled by sonority requirements on moras, but not by those placed on syllables. This is why the mora with the w label may be headed by a moraic segment that is not necessarily syllabic.

To sum up, asymmetries in sonority exhibited by the two moras of a bimoraic syllable, as well as the subset relation between them result, first, from independent sonority conditions on moras and on syllables, and second, from the subsyllabic metrical structure. To anticipate the discussion in a later part of this chapter, this result cannot be derived if we impose separate sonority conditions on the nucleus and the margin, and then derive the notion of mora on the basis of 'tree geometry'.

2.8 Further Predictions

In this section I will demonstrate that the two premises that serve as basis for the typology contribute to a number of valid predictions about subsyllabic structure. In subsection 2.8.1 we discuss types of closed syllables, and in subsection 2.8.2 we discuss types of heavy syllables.

2.8.1 Types of Closed Syllables

If the set of moraic segments is not always coextensive with the entire set of segments, then we need to reconsider the status of closed syllables with respect to weight. This issue is addressed in McCarthy 1979a, 1979b, and more recently in Hyman 1985. These studies explicitly argue for positing two types of closed syllables — those that are light and those that are heavy. Hyman represents this difference in the following fashion, and this is the representation I have adopted here:[18]

(90)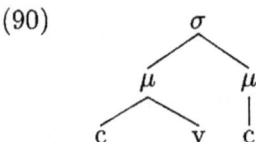

Sonority Constraints on Moras 47

(91)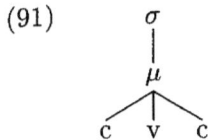

The framework I am developing here actually predicts this distinction. What is more, it also predicts in what range we should look for syllables of each type.

That we need both heavy and light closed syllables in our inventory follows directly from one particular generalization we propose in this chapter. Recall that the set of moraic segments is a subset of the segment inventory. Thus, any of the subsets in (92) can be selected as the set of moraic segments:

(92) Possible sets of syllabic segments:

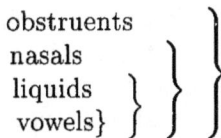

More precisely, the situation in which a language can have light closed syllables might potentially arise whenever the set of moraic segments is a *proper* subset of the segment inventory. Thus, we predict three types of cases, which are illustrated below by Khalkha Mongolian, English, and Kwakwala.[19]

Let us first look at a language like Khalkha Mongolian, whose set of moraic segments includes only vowels, as argued in 2.4:

(93) Khalkha Mongolian moraic segments:
vowels

Khalkha Mongolian has closed syllables. But since none of its consonants are moraic, none of the closed syllables that contain a short vowel will be heavy; that is, Khalkha Mongolian chooses the option mentioned in section 2.2. of adjoining an unmorified consonant to a preceding mora. Thus, closed syllables in Khalkha Mongolian will have the structure in (94):

(94)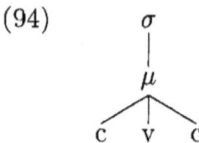

Next, let us consider a language like English, in which the set of moraic segments corresponds to the entire set of segments. In this case, all closed syllables have the structure in (95):

(95)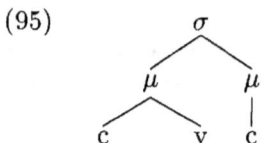

Finally, since the set of moraic segments may correspond to any of the subsets in (93) it is in principle possible to have both kinds of closed syllables in a single language. This situation is found in Kwakwala, where syllables closed with a sonorant are as in (96), and those closed with an obstruent (or a glottalized sonorant) as in (97):

(96)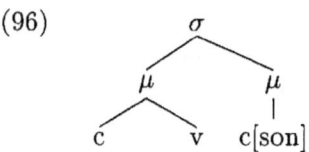

(97)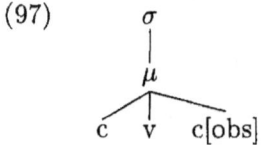

This is precisely the distinction we need for the languages presented in section 2.3. above, more precisely, for those that select the adjunction option: although both sonorants and obstruents can appear in the 'coda', only syllables closed with a sonorant are bimoraic. In other words, if a syllable is closed by a *moraic* consonant, its structure will have to be as in (96); but nonmoraic segments can only be attached to the preceding mora, if that option is available in the language.

Finally, we make a very strong prediction about those languages which have both types of closed syllables: that we will never find the situation in Kwakwala reversed, that is, heavy syllables closed with obstruents, and light syllables closed with sonorants.

(98)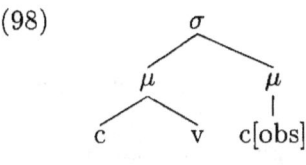

(99)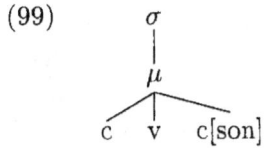

If the moraic set is a proper subset of the segment inventory, and if sets of moraic and syllabic segments always include the sonorous end of the scale, then the segments left out of the set will be at the nonsonorous rather than at the sonorous end.

2.8.2 Types of Heavy Syllables

One important result of this framework is that we derive in a straightforward manner the claim traditionally attributed to Trubetzkoy and Jakobson about the implicational relation between CVV and CVC syllables:

(100) If a language has (heavy) CVC syllables, it will also have (heavy) CVV syllables.

The implicational relation in (100) follows directly from the generalizations proposed herein, namely from Mor $\subseteq$ Seg, and from the fact that the segments at the sonorous end are always included in both the syllabic and the moraic set. Let us look again at possible sets of moraic segments:

(101) Possible sets of syllabic segments:

$$\left\{\left\{\left\{\begin{array}{l}\text{obstruents}\\ \text{nasals}\\ \text{liquids}\\ \text{vowels}\}\end{array}\right\}\right\}\right\}$$

We can think of a hypothetical language that has heavy syllables closed with obstruents. This will tell us that obstruents are in the set of moraic segments. If so, we will also know that this set includes all segments more sonorous than obstruents. Since vowels are also a member of this set, it then follows that if a language has heavy CVC syllables, it will also have heavy CVV syllables, which is exactly what Trubetzkoy's claim is. That is, we cannot have a language that has only CV and heavy CVC syllables because it is impossible to block the occurrence of vowels in the second mora: if consonants are in the set of moraic segments, vowels have to be there as well.

Moreover, it has been observed that the converse of (100) does not hold. In other words,

(102) If a language has (heavy) CVV syllables, it does not necessarily follow that it will also have (heavy) CVC syllables.

That the implication does not hold in the opposite direction follows from the generalization that Mor $\subseteq$ Syl. Let us therefore look at possible sets of syllabic segments:

(103) Possible sets of syllabic segments:

$$\left\{\left\{\left\{\begin{array}{l}\text{obstruents}\\ \text{nasals}\\ \text{liquids}\\ \text{vowels}\}\end{array}\right\}\right\}\right\}$$

After our discussion of Type Four languages, we are justified in saying that any of the subsets in (103) is a possible set of syllabic segments. Let us take a hypothetical language whose set of syllabic segments includes only vowels. On the basis of this we know, first, that vowels can appear under the s-labeled mora in the syllable:

(104)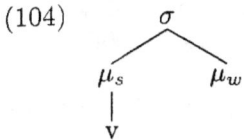

Next, since the set of syllabic segments is a subset of the set of moraic segments, it follows that every syllabic segment is also a moraic segment, that is, that vowels will also be admissible under the w-labeled mora:

(105)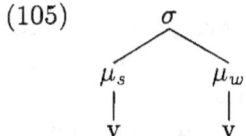

Since only syllabic segments can appear under the s-labeled mora, and since syllabic segments are also moraic, we derive the fact that all syllabic segments appear under the w-labeled mora as well.[20] But this is all we can predict: we have no way of determining whether any segments less sonorous than vowels are admissible under the second mora.

We thus derive what has been traditionally maintained to be true of syllable weight, that is, that, if a language has heavy CVC syllables, it will also have heavy CVV syllables. Note, however, that the relation between CVC and CVV syllables derived here concerns only syllable types. Under these assumptions, no claims are made about the status of long vowels in the language. The claims made here should be equally true of those languages that have contrastive vowel length, and of those that do not.

In other words, all we are saying is that if the heavy CVC syllable is one of the syllable types, then the CVV syllable is also available as a syllable type. This follows solely from the sonority requirements on certain subsyllabic positions on the one hand, and from the implicational relations between segments that differ in sonority, on the other. However, de Chene and Anderson 1979 explicitly claim that compensatory lengthening is possible only in languages with phonemic vowel length. In other words, they assume some kind of structure preservation governed by underlying contrasts, which affects the inventory of syllable types. From this it should follow that a language will have CVV syllables if and only if it has contrastive vowel length. It then further follows that Trubetzkoy's generalization should be rephrased as in (106):

(106) If a language has heavy CVC syllables, then it has a vowel length contrast.

First, it is not clear how the availability of a certain syllable type could affect the underlying inventory of segment types. A more likely direction of influence might be that the availability of phonemic vowel length affects the inventory of syllable types. But as we have just seen, no implication holds in this direction. Second, as pointed out in Hayes 1989b, we do find languages which have heavy CVC syllables, but no phonemic vowel length. Such a language is, for example, Ilocano, in which all vowel length contrasts are predictable, their sole source being compensatory lengthening. Thus a language may have noncontrastive vowel length as long as it possesses the relevant syllable type; the sources of noncontrastive vowel length are various phonological processes, one of which of course is compensatory lengthening.

In sum, whether a language will have the CVV syllable type depends on the availability of heavy syllables but not necessarily on vowel length contrasts. The necessary link comes from the implicational relations proposed in this chapter; that is, if moraic consonants are admissible in a certain subsyllabic position, then vowels will also be admissible in this position, since segments lower on the sonority scale imply those that are higher up, but not vice versa.[21]

2.9 Comparison with the Onset/Rhyme Representation

In the introductory section of this chapter we mentioned briefly the representation of subsyllabic structure in (107), with an onset/rhyme parsing and a derived notion of mora; throughout the chapter we used a different representation, the one in (108), with moras as primitives.

(107)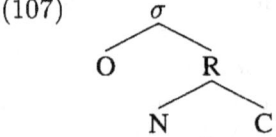

Sonority Constraints on Moras

(108) a.

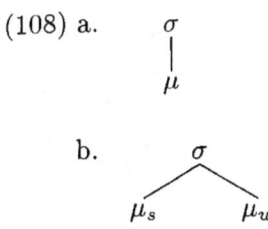

b.

In this section I will demonstrate the advantages of (108) over (107). As we have seen, the generalizations proposed in the present chapter are readily expressible in terms of the representation in (108). In what follows we will see that they are not as easy to express in terms of the other representation we have at hand.

The representation in (107) has access to two types of devices that I know of which could be utilized to express the relevant generalizations. The first one is tree geometry and the second coda constraints, to be discussed in subsections 2.9.1. and 2.9.2 respectively.

2.9.1 Tree Geometry

Under this approach, the principal assumption is that syllable weight is characterizable in structural terms. Hayes 1981 expresses the distinction between light and heavy syllables as in (109), that is, in terms of branchingness, or tree geometry:

(109) a.

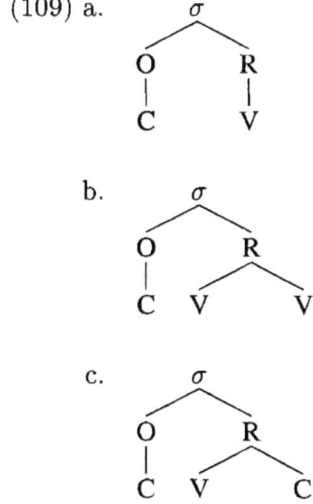

b.

c.

The branchingness is read either off the 'rhyme projection' of the syllable, making both CVV and CVC heavy; or off the nuclear or [+syllabic] projection, making only CVV syllables heavy. Other possible projections might be added, for example the [+sonorant] projection which would separate out CVV and CVS syllables as heavy, and CV and CVO syllables as light. However, further speculations along these lines bring us to the constraints approach, which I discuss in the next subsection.

Another proposal within this general research program is that of Levin 1985. Under this approach, the entire burden is placed on tree geometry, unaided by any segmental information. Levin introduces the notion of head of the syllable, in the spirit of the syntactic X' theory. The head of the syllable is the nucleus, which has several levels of projections, each of which can branch.

(110) N''
       |
       N'
       |
       N

Levin points to two levels of structure at which branching is relevant for weight or, as she expresses it, for accent rules: N', which dominates elements that appear in the coda, and N, which can dominate only the elements in the nucleus.[22] Thus, CVV syllables have the structure in (111)a, and CVC in (111)b:

(111) a.   N''
             |
             N'
             |
             N
            / \
           X   X

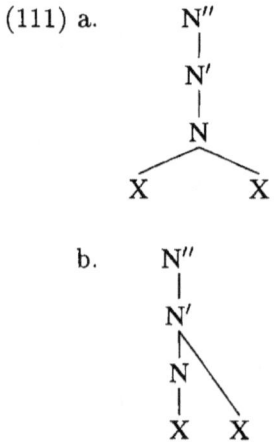

Note that Levin captures the implicational relation between CVV and CVC syllables: languages may vary as to whether the level of branchingness relevant for determining weight is the head of N″ (that is, N′ and N), or the head of N′ (that is, N). If a language picks the head of N″, then both CVC and CVV syllables will be heavy, since both N′ and N are heads of N″. And, if a language picks the head of N′, only CVV syllables will be heavy. Thus, Levin's framework derives the generalization that if a language has heavy CVC syllables it will also have heavy CVV syllables. Furthermore, this framework also captures that the converse of this generalization is not valid, that is, that heavy CVV syllables do not imply heavy CVC syllables.

Recall that in the framework I have developed in the preceding sections, CVC and CVV syllable types are just end points. As we have seen, in languages in which only a subset of consonants are moraic, we may have heavy CVV and CVS syllables but light CV and CVO syllables. However, this is precisely the situation that this framework excludes, as explicitly stated by Levin 1985:284:

> Having looked in vain for stress rules which require finer distinctions in sonority within the rhyme, it appears that the null hypothesis is that such rules do not exist. We take the strongest claim here and argue that such rules could not exist.

In other words, this framework rules out a system like Kwakwala. All finer distinctions would, according to Levin, require segmental information, and this is prohibited under her proposal. Given that any consonant can appear under the N′ node, it follows that certain consonants can be excluded from this position only by appealing to segmental information. Under the strong hypothesis that no segmental information is available at the syllabic projection, this system predicts that weight sensitive phenomena can distinguish either between CVV and CVC vs. CV syllables on the one hand, or CVV vs. CV and CVC on the other; and that these are the only weight distinctions that are needed.[23]

2.9.2 Constraints

We will now look at another mechanism that could be used to express the generalizations proposed in this chapter. This is the system of constraints, stated in terms of features, which are associated with the relevant subsyllabic nodes. Thus, this mechanism allows segmental information on the syllabic tier.

The subsyllabic positions that need to be constrained with respect to sonority are those dominated by the Rhyme node, that is, the Nucleus and the Coda. Constraints on the Nucleus will correspond to what we associated with the *s*-labeled mora; that is, this position will admit only those segments which are in the syllabic set. The Coda position, on the other hand, will be compatible only with the set of moraic segments.

I will discuss here two possible formal devices that can encode these constraints. First, we could place constraints on the nodes themselves, in the form of filters; Second, we could posit sets of moraic and syllabic segments in the grammar, and then associate these with particular nodes in essentially the way that this has been done for the representation with moras as primitives.

Let us start off with filters. Versions of this have been proposed in McCarthy 1979b, and more recently in Itô 1986. In a language like Kwakwala for example, the coda could be constrained as in (112) if we are using a positive filter, or as in (113) with a negative filter:

(112)   C
        |
        [+son]

(113) * C
         |
         [−son]

This mechanism can be extended to the nuclear position as well. Thus the sonority of the nucleus can be constrained by virtue of a positive filter, as in (114), or a negative filter, as in (114).

(114)   N
        |
        [+con]

(115) * N
         |
         [−con]

There are several problems with these filters, however. One

is the general problem associated with filters that we mentioned in 2.5.4: Nothing will prevent a negative filter like (116) which blocks the occurrence of sonorous segments in the coda although, as we have seen, only nonsonorous segments can be blocked in this position.

(116) * C
  |
  [+son]

But there is a further problem: recall that in addition to constraining the sonority of syllabic and moraic segments, we also need to express the subset relation that holds between them. But how are we to express this with only filters at our disposal? A relatively promising approach would be to have positive rather than negative filters, and then to define an implicational relation between the possible markings on the two positions, to be translated into the sonority scale. However, although the subset relation may eventually be expressible in terms of this notation, there will be no way of deriving it either from the features used, or from anything in the representation itself; in other words, it will have to be stipulated. The fact that this relation is repeated from language to language will be a pure accident under this account.

If we choose to posit sets of moraic and syllabic segments rather than filters, the constraint on the two subsyllabic positions can be stated as in (117):

(117) a. The Nucleus can dominate only those segments that appear in the set of syllabic segments.
  b. The Coda can dominate only those segments that appear in the set of moraic segments.

Since we have the sets of these segments stated in the grammar, we can now also state that these sets have to be in the subset relation. But again, this has to be stipulated, since there is no way of deriving this fact. The reason for this is that, under this representation, we are in effect constraining two unrelated subsyllabic positions. Thus there is no way of relating the constraints on one with those on the other in any nonarbitrary fashion. Recall that with moras as primitives of the representation, the constraints are placed on moras regardless of the moraic position we are constraining; this allows us to access the domain within which further constraints can be stated; in particular, the domain in which constraints on syllables can interact with those on moras.

In conclusion, the framework developed in this chapter makes two essential claims that any representation needs to capture: One is that syllabic and moraic segments stand in the subset relation, and the other is that sonority of segments and syllable weight are related in a nontrivial way. The tree geometry approach can capture the former, and the constraints approach can capture the latter. But neither of these representations is capable of capturing both, which is within the power of the representation with moras as primitives, as we saw in this chapter.

Notes

[1] This is also true of superheavy syllables, that is, those containing more than two moras.

[2] Note that this characterization does not depend in any crucial way on the representation we are utilizing. In the onset/rhyme type of representation, the syllabic segment appears under the nucleus, and the moraic one under the coda; both types of segments appear under the rhyme node, in accordance with the common assumption that only elements within the rhyme contribute to weight. In the representation with moras as primitives, the most sonorous segment dominated by the leftmost mora counts as syllabic, and the most sonorous segment under the second (or later) mora counts as moraic.

[3] The sonority scale given here does not include all the distinctions that languages may utilize. I will introduce more elaborate versions of the scale when needed.

[4] In (118) nasals and liquids are listed as being syllabic in English. See Mohanan 1986:29-34 for conditions under which this happens.

[5] Whether syllabic segments always have to be a *proper* subset of the segment inventory is a separate issue which I address in the next section.

[6] As suggested by Bill Poser, the statement in (118) may have to be rephrased as follows: the set of moraic segments is a subset of the segments permitted to appear in the coda. However, if there are independent constraints on the occurrence of segments at the syllable margin, then they will interact with the constraint in (118), and there will be no need to conflate several constraints into one.

[7] A third possibility would be that a language does not select the option of adjoining a nonmoraic consonant, nor does it have any special strategy to salvage such consonants, but I have not found any cases of this kind.

[8] According to Fischer-Jørgensen 1985, stød is realized phonetically as "a decrease in intensity and (often) pitch, in distinct speech ending in irregular vibrations (creaky voice), in very emphatic speech probably sometimes in a complete glottal closure."

[9] Stylistic shortening applies before oral, nonlateral sonorants.

[10] One of the ways to account for the failure of Stød Linking to apply to a structure like (118) could be in terms of inalterability as defined in Hayes 1986.

[11]Kenstowicz claims that short *o* appears only in foreign borrowings (see also Augustaitis 1964), and takes that as a basis for removing it from the inventory of the native sounds.

[12]Nasal infixes affect the tonal properties of the root; the mora they are associated with is linked to tone regardless of whether the nasal itself remains in the structure or gets lost. We could account for this by prelinking the nasal infix to a High tone in its underlying form.

[13]These rules apply postlexically, as evidenced by the resulting vowel qualities: the long vowels obtained this way are all lax.

[14]The examples in this subsection come from Boas 1947 and Grubb 1977. The page number after each examples refers to Boas 1947 unless stated otherwise.

[15]This generalization is first stated in Bach 1978. A number of examples given below also appear in this paper, although they originally appear in Boas 1947. The number next to each of the examples refers to Boas 1947.

[16]The transcription system used in this subsection is an adaptation of Boas' transcription system standardly used in work on American Indian languages.

[17]According to Chierchia 1982 *s* is allowed in the coda as well, while Vogel 1977 claims that *s* is always in the onset. Itô 1986 essentially follows Chierchia, but observes that *s* never occurs word finally, which makes its status somewhat ambiguous.

[18]In fact, Hyman uses the x symbol which represents what he refers to as 'weight units'; these 'weight units' correspond directly to moras, symbolized here as μ.

[19]While Hyman 1985 posits the difference between light and heavy closed syllables, this distinction does not follow from his framework.

[20]Note that this has direct bearing on syllabic consonants. In fact, one of the predictions of this framework is that all syllabic consonants will have to be moraic as well.

[21]Another potential counterargument against the claim advanced here comes from languages like Seneca, as described in Stowell 1979, in which CVC syllables act as heavy and CVV syllables as light. The important part of Stowell's claim is that vowel length is predictable in Seneca. However, according to Levin 1985:307-315, Seneca has two types of long vowels, those that are, and those that are not specified underlyingly; only the former behave as heavy for the purposes of stress rules. Thus CVV syllables

with underlyingly long vowels pattern with CVC syllables, and CVV syllables whose length is predictable do not. A possible reanalysis might be that the lengthening rule is ordered after stress assignment. Thus, the reason that CVV syllables appear to be light is that they in fact are light at the point when stress assignment applies.

[22] The coda position is available to any segment under Levin's proposal. However, this is not true of the nucleus, which seems to be independently constrained.

[23] Moreover, while Levin's framework predicts that a language may have light closed syllables, it also predicts that closed syllables are either all light or all heavy, and that no split like that found in Kwakwala can exist.

3

Formation of Moraic and Syllabic Structure

3.1 Introduction

The generalizations proposed in Chapter Two make crucial reference to the sonority of segments. In particular, it is argued that sonority within the syllable is constrained at more than one level: at the level of the mora, and at the level of the syllable. It is further claimed that sonority constraints placed on these units are stated independently of each other, which in its turn argues for the independence of structure at the two levels.

In this chapter I address directly the problem of sonority and its place in the grammar. Under the present approach, sonority is taken to be a derivative notion, dependent on the structural properties of segments. Next, I propose a morification algorithm which crucially depends on the relative sonority of segments; and a syllabification algorithm which operates on morified structure. Generating moras and syllables by two separate algorithms is justified by the fact that we derive a number of properties of subsyllabic structure that would otherwise have to be stipulated. This gives further justification to the initial move of treating moraic and syllabic structure as independent of each other.

3.2 Sonority

3.2.1 Sonority Scales

Generalizations about relative sonority of segments are justified by the natural classes that segments form for the purposes of various phonological processes. But although groupings of segments with respect to sonority have a clear empirical basis, it is less clear what formal mechanism can capture this in an appropriate fashion.

In the literature there are two classes of proposals regarding this issue. According to one class, relative sonority is derived from the major class features, as well as certain others that may be relevant (Lekach 1979 and Clements 1990). The second class of proposals are those that directly incorporate into the grammar the linear ordering of segments in terms of relative sonority, known as the sonority scale; positions on the scale are encoded by sonority indices assigned to individual segments (Hooper 1972, 1976, and Selkirk 1984a).

I will first comment briefly on the second class of proposals, in particular, the version in Selkirk 1984a. It is well known that the sonority scale replicates most of the subdivisions of segments that result from the major class features, in particular, the features SYLLABIC, SONORANT, and CONSONANTAL. From this Selkirk concludes that having both the sonority scale and the major class features in the grammar leads to redundancy; a natural move should therefore be to eliminate one or the other from the grammar. Selkirk resolves this conflict by eliminating the major class features, and by keeping the sonority scale as the multivalued feature *sonority* whose values are sonority indices, as in (1):

(1) Sonority Indices
    a   10
    e,o   9
    i,u   8
    r   7
    l   6
    m,n   5
    s   4
    v,z,ð   3
    f,θ   2
    b,d,g   1
    p,t,k   0.5

Note that this brings up two distinct issues; one is whether the sonority scale has the status of a universal, and the other is whether it has the status of a primitive. Of course, the assumption that the sonority scale is a primitive is justified only if it is also taken to be a universal, and this is obviously part of Selkirk's claim. But, of itself, the assumption that the sonority scale has a universal status leaves unresolved its status as a primitive. I will not concern myself with this issue here, and refer the reader to Clements 1990, where it is claimed that the major class features derive the universal sonority ranking not only in phonological but also in phonetic terms. In what follows I argue against the universal status of the sonority scale, and this leaves us with proposals which depend on the major class features for characterizing sonority.

I will focus here on one such proposal, that in Clements 1990. Clements' goal is to derive the relative sonority of segments from an adapted version of the major class features. He claims that the features in the table below, rather than certain others that have been proposed, yield hierarchically arranged classes of segments whose order corresponds to what is known as the sonority scale.[1]

(2)   O <   N <   L <   G <   V

−	−	−	−	+	syllabic(=V)
−	−	−	+	+	vocoid
−	−	+	+	+	approximant
−	+	+	+	+	sonorant
0	1	2	3	4	rank (relative sonority)

The number of plus symbols in each of the columns corresponds to the sonority index which expresses the relative sonority of the class of segments in question.

Note that one of the features utilized in this system is the feature SYLLABIC. In certain recent views on syllabification, the status of this feature has been brought into question (Levin 1985). As I will argue, the arrangement in (2) contains several redundancies; all these redundancies are due solely to the feature SYLLABIC.

First, note that vowels have the highest sonority index by virtue of the feature SYLLABIC ((4) obviously represents the situation in which only vowels can act as syllable peaks). The role that sonority indices play is of particular importance for the syllabification algorithm that Clements proposes. This algorithm crucially depends on sonority ranking in its choice of an appropriate syllable nucleus: given the arrangement in (2), only those segments whose sonority ranking equals 4 are treated as *syllabic* by the algorithm. Thus syllabicity is encoded, first, as a feature which contributes to sonority ranking; and second, as a property of those segments whose sonority ranks sufficiently high. This is reminiscent of using

Formation of Moraic and Syllabic Structure

the feature SYLLABIC both at the segmental and at the skeletal tier; as pointed out in Levin 1985, such repetitions create unnecessary redundancy which needs to be removed from the grammar.

Second, it is only by virtue of the feature SYLLABIC that vowels and glides are separated out into distinct sonority classes. If we adopt this, then for the sake of consistency, we would need to have separate sonority classes for syllabic and nonsyllabic liquids, syllabic or nonsyllabic nasals, etc. To avoid this, Clements tentatively proposes a revised table which leaves out glides, as in (3). (The table in (3) presents the extreme case of a language in which any segment can act as a syllable peak.) This seems to be the right move: if we assume that syllabicity is defined in terms of sonority, rather than the other way around, then the distinction between vowels and glides will not exist at the segmental level.

(3)
O <	N <	L <	V	
+	+	+	+	syllabic
−	−	−	+	vocoid
−	−	+	+	approximant
−	+	+	+	sonorant
1	2	3	4	rank (relative sonority)

Note however that this revision makes it obvious that the feature SYLLABIC is superfluous. In fact, the same relative ranking can be achieved even if the feature SYLLABIC is left out, as in (4).

(4)
O <	N <	L <	V	
−	−	−	+	vocoid
−	−	+	+	approximant
−	+	+	+	sonorant
0	1	2	3	rank (relative sonority)

In what follows, it will be claimed that, roughly in this form, the scale in (4) captures the sonority ranking that is needed universally.[2] But it will also be claimed that these are not all the sonority distinctions that need to be made.

3.2.2 Universal and Language-Specific Sonority Ranking

The question we will address in this section is whether the scale in (4) is a universally valid sonority scale; or more generally, whether it is possible to have a single, universally valid scale. I will argue that the scale in (4) is universal, to the extent that all languages need to make at least those distinctions that are defined by this scale. But, drawing upon the work of Steriade 1982 and Levin 1985, I will further argue that this scale is not sufficiently elaborate to yield all the distinctions that are needed empirically. In other words, while all the features utilized in this scale seem to be necessary for deriving relative sonority, they are not the only features that may contribute to this end.

However, Clements maintains that a scale like that in (2) has a universal status; or more generally, that whatever sonority scale is proposed, it should be treated as a universal. He rejects the alternative view that sonority scales may vary from language to language, on the following grounds (Clements 1990:296):

> The explanatory value of sonority theory lies in its ability to predict valid cross-linguistic generalizations. As soon as we allow the sonority scale to vary in its identity from one language to another, we seriously undermine its explanatory role by increasing the number of ways in which it can accommodate potential exceptions, thus reducing the number of cross-linguistic generalizations that it accounts for.

Moreover, Clements notes in an earlier version of this paper that allowing cross-linguistic variation in sonority scales may place undue burdain on the language learner. But, wxhile the point made by Clements is of major significance, his hypothesis may in fact be too strong. It would be difficult to assume that only those aspects of linguistic structure whose status is universal should be considered learnable. Various versions of parameterization have been proposed precisely in order to reconcile learnability with cross-linguistic variation. But allowing unconstrained language-particular departures from the universal sonority ranking can certainly give rise to problems concerning learnability.

With this in mind, let us now inspect the existent proposals for language-particular sonority scales. I will present in some detail the position advanced in Steriade 1982 and further developed in Levin 1985. According to Levin, there is a universal hierarchy of features that are relevant for determining sonority ranking, as in (5), rather than a universal sonority scale:[3]

(5)

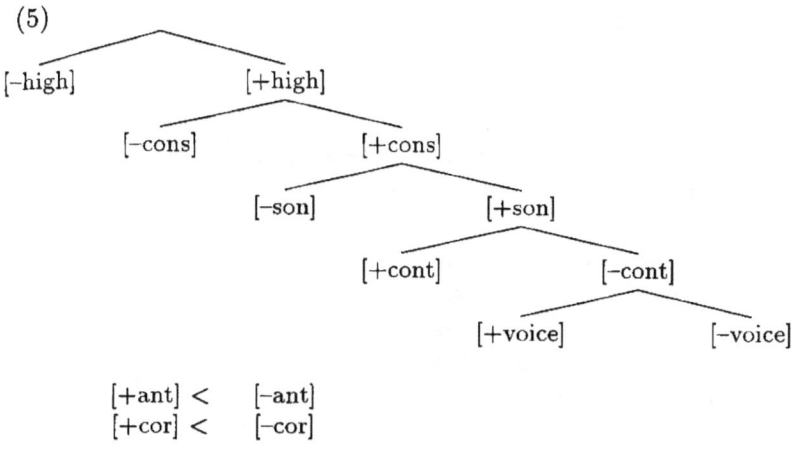

[+ant] < [−ant]
[+cor] < [−cor]

The hierarchy in (4) is part of the universal grammar, and serves as a basis for building language-particular sonority scales. In other words, being universal, this hierarchy of features has to be adhered to by individual languages; but languages may differ as to which of the features they choose to include in their language-particular scales, as long as they retain their relative hierarchical arrangement.[4]

Let us now return to Clements' objections against allowing variation in sonority scales. Recall that Clements has brought up the question of learnability — and given the fact that under Levin's proposal there are no constraints as to which of the features will be chosen by individual languages, this issue seems relevant here. The range from which the features are selected is large enough to present the learner with a nontrivial set of possibilities, and the actual segment clusters might be his/her only means of arriving at the right set.

But still, empirically it seems untenable to assume a single, universal sonority scale. We have seen that in Kwakwala glottalized segments are less sonorous than the unglottalized ones; and Levin shows that the feature CONTINUANT, for example, may be relevant for some languages but not for others; the scale proposed for Klamath utilizes this feature, while the one proposed for Chukchee does not.

(6) Klamath Sonority Scale
    w, y   [−cons]
    l, m, n   [+cons, +son]
    h, s   [+cons, −son, +cont]
    p, t   [+cons, −son, −cont, +ant]
    c, k, q   [+cons, −son, −cont, −ant]

(7) Chukchee Sonority Scale
    l, r   [+son, −nas]
    n, ñ   [+son, +nas, +cor]
    m   [+son, +nas, −cor]
    p, k, t, q [−son]

That is to say, we need to allow a certain degree of language specific flexibility in how elaborate the sonority scale may be. To accommodate this with the important point that unconstrained variation may easily open up the question of learnability, I will propose that a scale like (4), based entirely on the major class features, presents the universal core common to all languages; and that variation is expressed only in which of a small set of additional features may be turned on. Thus although the major class features are not the only features that participate in determining relative sonority, they belong to the common core which always has to be present. This parameterized version of the sonority scale is not in conflict with learnability, since it manipulates a minimal number of nonuniversal features, and is more compatible with the actual state of affairs, since it allows language-particular variation.

In contrast, part of Levin's claim is that none of the features appearing in the hierarchy in (5) is needed universally. That is to say, any of those features may fail to appear in at least some language-particular scales. But when we look at the sonority scales that result from this hierarchy, one feature that is unexceptionally selected is the feature SONORANT. By including the feature SONORANT into every language-particular scale, Levin tacitly recognizes at least its special, if not its universal, status. Under our approach, it is no accident that this feature is repeatedly selected by languages, since we have granted it the universal status. However, we also consider the feature CONSONANTAL as belonging to the universal set, although this view is not shared by Steriade and Levin. As will be argued in the next subsection, leaving out

Formation of Moraic and Syllabic Structure

the feature CONSONANTAL gives rise to unconstrained variation in individual scales.

3.2.3 Relative Sonority Ranking

In the previous subsection I proposed a set of features that sonority ranking is universally grounded upon. I also proposed that, in addition, some other features are selected on a language-particular basis. If we adopt the set of features proposed by Levin, then, under our revision, those that are needed universally will be the features CONSONANTAL and SONORANT (and, following Clements, APPROXIMANT as well). We are then left with the features listed in (8) as relevant to sonority ranking, in addition to those taken here to be needed universally:

(8)   CONTINUANT
      VOICING
      ANTERIOR
      CORONAL

Note that under the present approach all these features belong to the residual set that languages may or may not select from. But in what sense are all the segment classes created by these features relevant for sonority? In the present context, sonority ranking serves primarily to distinguish between nonmoraic, moraic, and syllabic segments. Since the moraic or syllabic status of a segment is clearly based on sonority alone, any class of such segments also picks out a sonority class in the language in question. As we have seen, the number of classes needed for this purpose is relatively small; in addition to the universally needed features, we have to add the feature GLOTTALIZED for Kwakwala, and CONTINUANT for Italian. More generally, I will propose that, under this view of sonority, the only features relevant for sonority distinctions are the so-called stricture features, that is, those that affect the opening of the air passage. Under this view, both the feature VOICING and the place features should be excluded from the residual set. The features CONTINUANT and GLOTTALIZED are the only features that can be retained.

But why is it that Steriade and Levin consider all the features listed in (8) relevant to sonority? These features are introduced due to the commonly held assumption that sonority ranking is responsible for characterizing tautosyllabic clusters in terms of the so-called minimal sonority distance (Hooper 1976, Steriade 1982, Selkirk 1984a, Levin 1985, Clements 1990). Minimal distance constraints have been posited to account for the fact that the sonority curve formed by the syllable is not sufficient to account for all constraints on clusters: thus two consonants may be prohibited from appearing in a sequence, although their relative sonority conforms to the general sonority requirements of the syllable. To take an example from Kiparsky 1979, while *blick* is a possible sequence in English, *bnick* is not, although neither violates the sonority constraints. The common explanation has been that the sonority classes that *b* and *n* belong to are not sufficiently distant from each other, while those of *b* and *l* are. This has been taken as motivation for finer and finer cuts within the sonority space of particular classes. Furthermore, this has also motivated the use of features like VOICING or CORONAL for determining sonority ranking. For example, Steriade 1982:98 includes the feature VOICING into the sonority scale of Greek, and the feature CORONAL into the sonority scale of Latin, and claims that this difference is sufficient to characterize the initial clusters in the two languages.

It is not clear, however, that all tautosyllabic sequencing should be accounted for in terms of sonority. In fact, it might well be that at least some of the sequencing facts can be attributed to certain other principles that are operative in language. Minimal sonority distance seems to incorporate requirements for minimal dissimilarity, which need not at all be related to sonority sequencing. Kiparsky 1979 proposed to handle the *bnick/blick* facts by appealing to a constraint on stop sequences:

(9)   * [[–cont] [–cont]]$_\sigma$

Most sonority scales to be found in the literature have been motivated by the minimal distance facts. But if we can account for minimal distance in some other terms, along the lines proposed by Kiparsky for example, then it appears that the features CONTINUANT and GLOTTALIZED should be sufficient to account for language-particular sonority distinctions. This set of features is small enough to avoid the learnability problems discussed above. Furthermore, the choice of these rather than certain other features is justified by the principles to be proposed here for dividing up

Formation of Moraic and Syllabic Structure

the sonority space: they never create the kinds of undesirable situations to be described below.

We will now address directly the issue of the range within which we should allow the modification of the universal sonority ranking within individual languages. The set of feature that we claim to be universally needed for characterizing sonority divide up the entire segment space into the following sonority classes:

(10) *obstruents*   *nasals*   *liquids*   *vowels*

Thus if two segments a and b belong to different sonority classes, their relative sonority ranking is determined universally by the relative sonority ranking of their respective classes; and, if a and b belong to the same class, they will be of equal sonority.

But how is this arrangement modified in individual languages? I will propose that modifications can affect only those segments which are ranked by the universal scale as being equal in sonority. In other words, the additional features can introduce further subdivisions within each of the classes, thus creating finer sonority rankings among segments. Note that this excludes cases of reversing, or conflating, the sonority of segments which belong to different sonority classes. Given this proposal, the creation of such cases should not be within the power of mechanisms responsible for language-particular variation.

However, several such proposals have been made in the literature. This situation arises for example in what Steriade 1982 proposes to be the sonority scales for Sanskrit (p.329) and for Common Greek (p.348). In both cases, glides rank lower in sonority than liquids, which is in conflict with what I propose to be the universal ranking. However, the scales proposed by Steriade are meant to account for the minimal distance phenomena, which under the present assumptions do not necessarily depend on sonority.[5]

We have seen that one of the features on the universal feature hierarchy proposed by Levin is CONSONANTAL; however, by excluding this feature from the set that determines sonority ranking we place liquids and vowels into the same sonority class, as in (11):

(11) *obstruents*   *nasals*   *liquids+vowels*

Once they are in the same class, liquids and glides are treated as being equal in sonority universally, and therefore reorderable on a language-particular basis. Such reorderings are not only undesirable but also unnecessary, as long as they are motivated solely by minimal distance facts. Liquids pattern much more naturally with consonants than they do with vowels, and the ranking in (11) fails to capture this intuition. In sum, language-particular sonority distinctions should respect universal sonority classes, as schematized in (12):

(12)   obstruents   nasals   liquids   vowels

Even with the constraint against what are proposed here to be universally valid classes, we still do not resolve the problem of how to introduce further, language-specific cuts within the space set by the major ones. In particular, even if we take the situation in (12) as our point of departure, there is still a danger of deriving different relative rankings of segments for different languages. In order to clarify this point, let us see how the sonority space occupied by obstruents can be further subdivided. We will take three hypothetical languages, whose inventories of obstruents are identical, and include, say, *t, d, s,* and *z*.

Language A utilizes only the universally needed features for determining sonority, and happens not to select any other feature on a language-particular basis. In this case, all obstruents will rank equally, as shown in (13):

(13)   Language A
       t, d, s, z

Language B, however, happens to select the feature CONTINUANT in addition to the features needed universally. Note that here stops are less sonorous than fricatives:

(14)   Language B
       t, d
       s, z

In Language C, which selects the feature VOICING, we will get the following ranking:

(15) Language C
      t, s
      d, z

Note that in Language B s is more sonorous than d, while in Language C the situation is reversed, that is, d is more sonorous than s. The framework developed by Steriade and Levin allows variation of this kind, and I would like to claim that such variation is undesirable. It seems in fact that either the feature CONTINUANT or the feature VOICING should be excluded from the set of features that contribute to sonority. The features that are the universal basis of sonority never create such conflicts; nor does the feature CONTINUANT, which is also a stricture feature.[6] On the other hand, the feature VOICING does create conflicts in sonority ranking, which we take as sufficient grounds for leaving it out of the set of features related to sonority, since no motivation other than the minimal distance phenomena has been offered for keeping it in this set.

In view of this, I propose that language-specific modifications should be constrained in the following fashion: given two segments a and b, which belong to the same sonority class, we should not have the situation of a being more sonorous than b in one language, and less sonorous than b in another. Of course, a finely grained universal scale would resolve this problem. In section 3.3 we will see how this constraint can be derived under the present assumptions.

3.3 Proposal

In this section I propose a method for encoding relative sonority of segments without utilizing sonority indices. Recall that the basic motivation for positing sonority indices has been to compute minimal distance. But if minimal distance facts are not directly related to sonority, as will be proposed here, then we lose this particular motivation for this device. Later in this chapter, I suggest that there might be a way of dealing with minimal distance requirements without positing sonority indices.

But if we do not need sonority indices for minimal distance facts, then sonority ranking no longer has to be expressed in terms of a sonority scale with indices assigned as values to individual classes of segments. I elaborate on this in the present section. In particular, I will demonstrate that we do not need the sonority scale and the integer values that commonly go with it in order to compute relative sonority of segments.

In the following discussion I will follow Levin 1985 in assuming that sonority can be computed from a hierarchically arranged set of features. But while I agree with Levin that the hierarchical arrangement of features is relevant for relative sonority, I do not agree that this needs a special statement in the grammar. I will argue here that the feature geometry of the melody (Clements 1985), motivated on independent grounds, possesses the right hierarchical arrangement for the purposes of sonority.

One thing that has not been discussed in the previous section is the method whereby the sonority ranking of a segment is computed from the scale in (4), which is repeated below:

(16) O < N < L < V
       −   −   −   +   vocoid
       −   −   +   +   approximant
       −   +   +   +   sonorant
       0   1   2   3   rank (relative sonority)

The method consists in counting the number of plus values in the matrix. Counting the plus values, rather than, say, the minus values, might be motivated if one assumes a particular version of the markedness theory, but Clements is not explicit on this issue.[7] This suggests that the plus value should not be assigned any special status that would distinguish it from the others.

My alternative will be to couch this proposal within the theory of underspecification, following Levin 1985. As pointed out by Levin, this move is motivated by the fact that information about sonority is needed at an early point in the lexical phonology. In other words, we need to have access to sonority information before the default features are introduced into the representation. As a consequence, the only relevant distinction will be presence vs. absence of feature specifications; it will be of no significance what particular value the specification present in the structure corresponds to. For example, under this proposal it is no longer necessary to use the feature VOCOID in the scale in (16). The better known feature CONSONANTAL will perform the same function. The table this gives us is as in (17):

Formation of Moraic and Syllabic Structure

(17)   O < N < L < V
                                       − consonantal
                       +   +   approximant
           +   +   +   sonorant

In the previous section it was claimed that while the major class features may not be the only ones needed for determining sonority, they are the ones that are needed universally. In what follows I will show that the feature geometry of the melody, as proposed in McCarthy 1988 (and motivated on independent grounds) provides precisely the groupings of features that we need for sonority ranking.

Under the SPE theory (Chomsky and Halle 1968), where all features associated with a segment belong to the same feature bundle, the task of separating out the set of features needed for sonority is less than straightforward, for obvious reasons. But under the feature geometry approach, we can separate out a subgroup of features if they pattern together with respect to phonological processes. In fact, all the features in table (17) belong to the class of degree of closure features, as Sagey 1986 calls them, or stricture features, to use the term introduced in Schein and Steriade 1986. According to several approaches, in particular Sagey 1986, Schein and Steriade 1986, and McCarthy 1988, these features should be associated directly with the root node. Sagey 1986 simply treats the root node as their class node:

(18)   root
        laryn   supralaryn   cons   cont   son

Schein and Steriade 1986 also associate the stricture features with the root node, but in a different fashion: these features label root nodes directly. The motivation given for this is that they never occasion partial assimilation.

(19)   root [cons,cont,son]
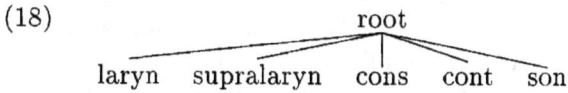
       laryn   supralaryn

Finally, McCarthy 1988 argues that the feature CONTINUANT can both spread and delink; he then distinguishes between those stricture features which do not spread or delink, that is CONSONANTAL and SONORANT, and those that do spread or delink such as CONTINUANT. The former label the root node, while the latter treat the root node as their class node:

(20)   root [cons,son]

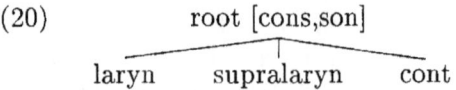

laryn   supralaryn   cont

If we add the feature APPROXIMANT to the group of features labeling the root node, as in (21), we get all the features relevant for the sonority ranking at one place; furthermore, no features other than these label the root node, which separates out exactly the subclass of features we need.

(21)   root [cons,son,approx]

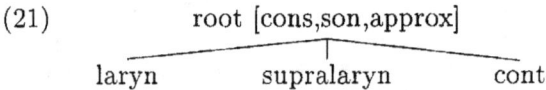

laryn   supralaryn   cont

As proposed above, this particular subclass of features is needed universally; certain other features may be selected on a language-particular basis, the feature CONTINUANT being one of them. We come to this issue later in the section.

Having separated the set of features that are universally utilized for sonority distinctions, we can now address the question of sonority ranking: how do we compute the relative ranking of individual segments? I will claim here that there is no need to do this by assigning integer values. The effect of creating implicationally related classes will be achieved equally well by appealing to the notions of extension and proper extension, introduced in Gazdar and Pullum 1982 (see also Gazdar, Klein, Pullum and Sag 1985) to define the ordering of category matrices in terms of their information content.[8]

(22) Extension:
      Segment A is an extension of segment B iff all feature specifications in B are also found in A.

(23) Proper Extension:
      Segment A is a proper extension of segment B iff all feature

specifications in B are also found in A, and A has at least one feature specification not found in B.

We can in fact say that, universally, extension makes reference only to the root node and its labels. It then follows that vowels are a proper extension of all other segments, that liquids are a proper extension of all segments other than vowels, and that nasals are a proper extension of obstruents. Thus, extension fully captures relative sonority of segments, as stated in (24):

(24) Segment A is more sonorous than segment B iff A is a proper extension of B.

We have assumed that the root node universally participates in determining relative sonority. We can further assume that other nodes can participate as well, but that this will happen on a language-particular basis. Thus the feature CONTINUANT, for example, might be added to distinguish between classes of obstruents and the node GLOTTALIZED will interfere both with obstruents and with sonorants. More generally, these nodes might add information on top of what is already determined by the root node. This is precisely what Steriade 1982:99 intuitively expresses by saying that "the hierarchy of features present on a scale is fixed universally. We could not set up a scale in which continuancy distinctions take precedence over obstruency distinctions."

In the next section I show how the notion of relative sonority, expressed in terms of extension, is utilized by algorithms that build prosodic structure.

3.4 Moraic and Syllabic Structure

In most approaches to syllable structure, it has been assumed that syllabification algorithms operate on segments linked to the skeletal tier — either the CV tier or, as proposed in Levin 1985, the X tier. Under the present approach, neither the CV nor the X tier is assumed; rather the subsyllabic timing tier corresponds to moraic structure. In its turn, moraic structure has a number of predictable properties, and is therefore also derivable by phonological mechanisms.

3.4.1 Morification

Let us start with the morification algorithm. This algorithm will operate on an unmorified, ordered string of root nodes. The information that this algorithm will crucially depend on is the degree of sonority of individual segments, and I will have to assume that this information is readily available to the algorithm. As argued in the preceding section, relative sonority is expressible in terms of extension, and we will make reference to this notion here as well. Before offering a formalized account of this process, I first show how morification functions.

As an illustration, we will first look at the morification of an English string. Recall that English is a Type One language, that is, that any of its segments can be moraic; but as we will see, being in the set of moraic segments is not in itself sufficient for a segment to be capable of licensing a mora.

Let us take the string *any*, rendered phonologically as *eni*. A left to right scan would stop at *e*, the first moraic segment in the string, and link it to a mora:

(25)   μ
        |
        e   n   i

In this case it seems sufficient that this segment is in the set of English moraic segments; but an additional condition is that the eligible moraic segment is not immediately followed by a *more* sonorous segment, and this condition is satisfied in (25). In (26) and (27) for example, the algorithm will not link *r* or *l* to a mora although these segments are members of the set, because each is followed by a more sonorous segment. But the following vowel can be morified because it satisfies both conditions: it is a member of the set, and it is followed by a less sonorous segment.

(26)   μ
            ╱|
           r e   d   i

(27)   μ
              ╱|
           b l i   n   k

Formation of Moraic and Syllabic Structure

Note that l does get linked to a mora when it satisfies both conditions, as in (29):

(28)

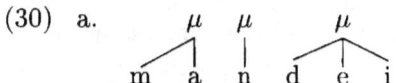

What we said so far can be stated in a morification algorithm of the following form:[9]

(29) Morification (first approximation)
Given a sequence S of unlinked segments $s_1, s_2, ..., s_i, ..., s_n$, link S to μ iff
  a. s_i is more sonorous than s_{i-1}
  b. s_n is a member of the set of moraic segments
  c. s_n is *not* immediately followed by a more sonorous segment.

An important result is that strings like *Monday* and *betray* will be morified as in (30) rather than, say, (31):

(30) a.

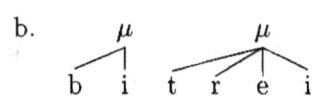

  b.

  b i t r e i

(31) a. *

  m a n d e i

  b. *

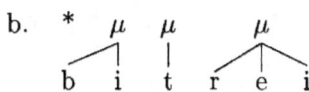

In (31)a n cannot be skipped over since it is eligible to be linked to a mora; and in (31)b t should not have been linked to a mora since it is followed by a more sonorous segment.

We will now revise the algorithm, by incorporating into it the notion of extension introduced in the previous section. The revised version of the algorithm is as in (32):

(32) Morification
Given a sequence S of unlinked segments $s_1, s_2, ..., s_i, ..., s_n$, link S to μ iff
  a. s_i is an extension of s_{i-1}
  b. s_n is a member of the set of moraic segments
  c. s_n is an extension of the immediately following segment, if any.

Note that Clause c covers both those cases where the following segment is less sonorous, and those where no segment follows; futhermore, we no longer have a negative statement, as in the previous version of the algorithm.

We have seen how the proposed morification algorithm operate Type One language, in which all segments are potentially moraic. But this algorithm is equally applicable to other language types, precisely because it leaves unspecified the information which segments will be moraic. Clause b is interpreted on a language-particular basis, by making reference to the set of moraic segments that the language in question possesses. Thus, this same algorithm will be equally operative in any other language type. To illustrate this, let us see how this algorithm operates in a language like Kwakwala.

We will take two Kwakwala forms, both having an initial closed syllable. In (33) the initial syllable is closed with a moraic consonant. The algorithm will first morify ə and the preceding consonant; then it will link l to a mora. And finally, the algorithm will morify the sequence xa.

(33)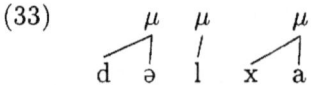

Observe now what happens when the initial syllable is closed with a nonmoraic consonant. The consonant/vowel sequence will be morified as in the preceding example. The sequence xa will be morified next, and the consonant s will remain unmorified, since x is not its proper extension.

(34)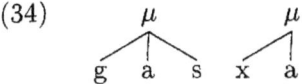

The consonant *s* will be adjoined to the left (since Kwakwala allows this option, see 2.2 and 2.8.1), and create a light closed syllable.

More generally, the algorithm groups together maximally long substrings of ascending, or level, sonority; in the latter case, the substring consists of only one member.

3.4.2 Syllabification

The syllabification algorithm operates on moraic structure, grouping moras into syllables. This algorithm has at least two modes of operation that languages may select. First, it can map every single mora to a syllable, that is, it can operate in a one-to-one fashion, as in (35):

(35) $\sigma\ \ \sigma\ \ \sigma\ \ \sigma$
$\ \ \ \ \ |\ \ \ \ |\ \ \ \ |\ \ \ \ |$
$\ \ \ \ \mu\ \ \mu\ \ \mu\ \ \mu$

Second, this algorithm may operate in a one-to-many fashion, relating a syllable node with one or more moras, which obtain *s w* labeling, as in (36):

(36)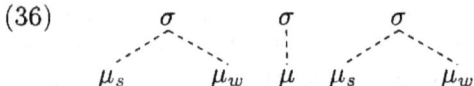

This will distinguish between those languages which have only monomoraic syllables, and those whose syllables may contain more than one mora.

Let us first focus on the situation sketched in (36). We can again turn to a language like English, in which we find an asymmetry between moraic and syllabic segments. The syllabification algorithm will link a syllable node to a mora (assigning this mora the *s* label if it is not the only one in the syllable) only under certain minimal sonority requirements, in particular, if the mora in question contains at least one segment of the required sonority. If not, this mora will only be eligible for adjunction to an already existent syllable node, and for obtaining a *w* label, which is assigned freely. This is illustrated in (37):

(37)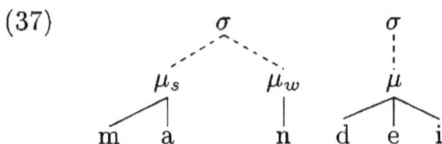

Furthermore, if the algorithm groups more than one mora into a syllable, the *s w* labeling it assigns reflects also the relative sonority of the two moras: the *w* mora can never be more sonorous than the *s* mora.

The one-to-one mapping is found in languages in which syllables contain at most one mora, that is, in which all syllables are light. Note, however, that a language which has only monomoraic syllables does not necessarily have coextensive sets of syllabic and moraic segments. This mapping will thus proceed in different fashion in those languages whose syllabic and moraic segments are coextensive, and in those in which the former are a proper subset of the latter. In order to make this point, I list the language types in (38):

(38)   a.   Type One: Syl ⊂ Mor = Seg
        b.   Type Two: Syl = Mor ⊂ Seg
        c.   Type Three: Syl ⊂ Mor ⊂ Seg
        d.   Type Four: Syl = Mor = Seg

Types Two and Four have coextensive sets of moraic and syllabic segments, and the algorithm will be able to map the syllable nodes into any mora without the danger of this mora not being headed by a syllabic segment. However, the situation is different in Type One and Type Three languages, where the set of syllabic segments is a proper subset of the moraic ones. In this case, the mapping will not affect every single mora — but rather, only those moras licensed by a segment which is both moraic and syllabic. For example, we can conceive of a language in which only vowels are syllabic, but in which both vowels and sonorant consonants are moraic. One possibility is that only those moras headed by a vowel (represented as v) are part of the mapping, while those headed by a sonorant consonant (represented as s) are not:[10]

(39)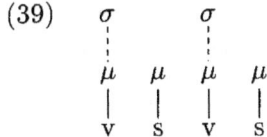

A further possibility is for the one-to-one mapping to proceed in a 'blind' fashion. The task of salvaging the syllables without a proper sonority peak would then be delegated to some repair mechanism, for example epenthesis, as is the case in Bulgarian, discussed in Chapter Four.

But what happens if a language with underlying vowel length has the syllabification algorithm which operates in a one- to-one fashion? Cases of this kind are possible, as I will argue; the resulting property of such languages will be to have long vowels but no diphthongs. The reason for this is that the algorithm will treat the configuration in (40) as special, and will not operate in its regular fashion:

(40)

More precisely, the algorithm will not be able to 'split' a long vowel between two syllables, and will have to include both moras linked to it into the same syllable, as shown in (41):

(41)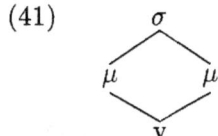

However, (bimoraic) diphthongs can only be created if the algorithm allows one-to-many mappings, which then accounts for the absence of diphthongs in languages with a one-to-one syllable to mora mapping which also possess phonemic vowel length. An example of such a language is Serbo-Croatian, which is discussed in Chapter Five.

To summarize the preceding discussion, the syllabification algorithm is extremely simple: all the checking that needs to be done is that the s label be assigned to a mora headed by a syllabic segment. No checking needs to be done on the w labeled moras, whose well-formedness has been taken care of by the morification algorithm.

3.5 Consequences

3.5.1 Sonority Sequencing Constraints and the Syllable Contact Law

It has generally been observed that the syllable forms a sonority curve: its most sonorous segment is the nucleus, which is flanked by sequences of segments whose sonority decreases towards the margins. This property of the syllable follows directly from the morification and syllabification algorithms proposed here.

Recall that the morification algorithm groups segments into sequences of ascending sonority. This sonority property of the mora will then naturally extend to the syllable, since the syllable is only a special grouping of moras. The rising sonority of its initial mora will create the ascending sonority curve at the left margin of the syllable. Thus, the morification algorithm is sufficient to account for the ascending part of the syllable curve. The descending part, on the other hand, will be accounted for by the syllabification algorithm. Recall that the two moras of the bimoraic syllable exhibit an asymmetry regarding their relative sonority. This is expressed in the present framework by the $s\ w$ labeling on the two subsyllabic constituents:

(42)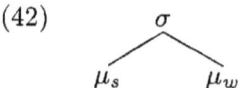

That is, the weak mora can be either equally or less sonorous than the strong one, which potentially creates a descending curve. Note that this situation can never create an ascending curve, which is exactly the result we need.

The morification algorithm also derives what is known as the syllable contact law (Hooper 1976, Clements 1990): the initial segment in a syllable is less sonorous than the final segment of the immediately preceding syllable. In fact, this is the only possible result, given that our morification algorithm creates sequences of ascending sonority. To be more specific, two adjacent segments a and b will belong to different moras only if a is more sonorous than

Formation of Moraic and Syllabic Structure 85

b; if a is less sonorous than b, the two segments create a sequence of ascending sonority, and will therefore be grouped into a single mora. This property of moras will extend to syllables, since boundaries between moras are potentially boundaries between syllables.

Clements 1990 observes that although the two subparts of the syllable curve are roughly symmetrical due to the descent in sonority towards syllable margins, the left-hand subpart of the curve is generally steeper than the right-hand one. This property also follows from the general framework set up here. First, it follows from the syllable contact law, which we account for in terms of the morification algorithm. Second, it follows from the proposal that each language has a set of moraic segments, which can potentially be a proper subset of the segment inventory. This automatically results in a higher sonority of the right syllable margin compared to the left one.

3.5.2 Minimal Distance Constraints

In the approach developed here there is no direct way of capturing the facts of minimal distance (Hooper 1976, Selkirk 1984a, Steriade 1982, Clements 1990). Although I will not discuss this problem in detail, I propose to show, briefly, that at least some of the cases for which constraints of this kind have been proposed follow from the morification algorithm proposed here, more specifically, from what we defined in (22) and(23) as extension. As will be shown here, the mechanisms we have at our disposal yield the right results only when combined with other constraints that are independently needed in the grammar.

We will examine one case for which minimal distance constraints have been proposed. No use will be made of integer values as markers of sonority, or of intervening intervals as a measure of minimal distance.

The case we look at is Latin as analyzed in Steriade 1982.

(43) Latin Sonority Scale (Steriade 1982)
  [−son, −cont, −cor] :   p, k, b, g
  [−son, −cont, +cor] :   t, d
  [−son, +cont, −cor] :   f
  [−son, +cont, +voice] :   s
  [+son, −cont, +nas, −con] : m
  [+son, −cont, +nas, +con] : n
  [+son, +cont, −nas, +lat] : l
  [+son, +cont, −nas, −lat] : r

The minimal distance requirement for Latin is 6 intervals which, according to Steriade, excludes clusters in (44)a, but allows those in (44)b:

(44) a. *pn, *fr, *tl, *dl
      b. stop − liquid

The feature CORONAL is crucially responsible for the scale in (43). We claimed earlier that this feature is not a member of the class of features that affect sonority. We will now see that this feature is indeed responsible for the constraints on clusters we find in Latin. However, there is no need to account for these constraints in terms of sonority.

Let us start with the prohibited clusters *tl and *dl. One property of these clusters is that they share *two* features, CONTINUANT and CORONAL. The permitted clusters such as *tr, dr* or *pl* share at most one feature. Furthermore, clusters such as *sn* and *fn* will be excluded due to extension: fricatives are marked for the feature CONTINUANT, while nasals are marked for the feature SONORANT, so that neither class can be the extension of the other. Thus, only those sequences are permitted which share at most one feature, and which stand in the relation of extension.

While this account is not exhaustive, it is suggestive of how one can deal with minimal distance facts, which might well be conditions on dissimilarity, and as such unrelated to sonority.

Notes

[1] Clements introduces the feature APPROXIMANT, which is not traditionally listed among the major class features. The role of this feature is to separate out nasals and liquids. In particular, Clements claims that both nasals and *l* are noncontinuant; but unlike nasals, *l* is an approximant, and thus patterns together with *r* and vowels.

[2] In a later section, I will replace the feature VOCOID by CONSONANTAL.

[3] This type of proposal is originally due to Lekach 1979.

[4] The features ANTERIOR and CORONAL can be introduced at any point in the hierarchy.

[5] Another case in the literature which would need a scale with *l* ranking higher than glides is Hankamer and Aissen's 1974 analysis of assimilation in Pali. The Pali case appears to be a serious counterexample to the present claim, if it indeed is a case of sonority-driven consonant assimilation. I believe, however, that this case will lend itself to a reanalysis in terms of feature delinking. A general constraint on consonant clusters in Pali is that they have to be doubly linked; if we assume that members of consonant clusters with singly linked features undergo delinking, a number of facts can be accounted for without any need to refer to the sonority scale.

[6] The feature GLOTTALIZED may have this effect; however, it also seems that this feature alters the stricture properties of a segment.

[7] Clements 1990:17 says that plus-specifications for the features taken to be relevant to sonority "have the effect of increasing the perceptibility of a sound with respect to otherwise similar sounds having a minus-specification, in the sense that they contribute toward increasing its loudness (a function of intensity), or toward making its formant structure more prominent." However, this does not seem to be in the nature of plus, but not of minus, values; if we replace the feature VOCALIC with CONSONANTAL, then the minus value will have all the properties that Clements attributes to the plus value.

[8] This notion comes from unification-based formalisms (Shieber 1986), and corresponds to a superset relation. Its converse is the notion of subsumption, comparable to a subset relation (see Shieber 1986:14-16).

⁹The morification algorithm could also be construed as a two-step process, consisting first in linking a moraic segment to a mora, and then in right-adjoining the segments to the left of the moraic one, as long as they are of descending sonority. This is reminiscent of the two rules that Kahn 1976 posits for selecting the syllable peak, and then linking the onset consonants to it.

¹⁰In this case I will assume adjunction of the moraic but non-syllabic segment to the preceding mora, if that mechanism is available; or stray erasure, if it is not (see Itô 1986).

4

The Mora as a Prosodic Unit

4.1 Introduction

In this chapter[1] my intention is to argue for the prosodic status of the mora, which is a direct consequence of how the algorithms proposed in Chapter Three build prosodic structure. There I proposed two independent algorithms — one that creates moras and one that creates syllables. Being independent, these algorithms may in principle operate at different points in the derivation. Since the syllabification algorithm applies on morified structure, we get two logical possibilities: the creation of syllables may either be simultaneous with, or come after the creation of moras.

This is in conflict with the commonly held assumption that syllables ought to be present from an early point in the derivation, that is, that syllabification proceeds in cyclic fashion, starting with the earliest cycle (see Kiparsky 1979, Steriade 1982, Levin 1985). It will be claimed here that this mode of creation is necessary for moras but not for syllables. Given the logical possibilities just listed, my framework predicts cases of languages in which the two algorithms do not operate simultaneously, that is, cases of languages in which syllables are created at a later point than moras. Bulgarian provides exactly this kind of case: it has moras but no syllables present at the earliest lexical level. The case of Bulgarian will thus show that moras and syllables need not be co-present at all levels of the lexical phonology.[2]

Moreover, this case demonstrates that moras are not only subsyllabic constituents but also prosodic units. The reason for this is that segments need to be prosodically licensed at all stages of the derivation, including the earliest ones. This is necessary in order to avoid stray erasure, as stated by the following principle proposed in Itô 1986:

(1) *Prosodic Licensing:* Phonological units have to be incorporated into (higher) prosodic structure (modulo extraprosodicity). [Itô 1986]

Itô assumes that prosodic licensing is performed by syllables (Itô 1986). But as I will show, Bulgarian syllables are formed relatively late in the lexical component; the theory, therefore, forces us to assume that the syllable is not the prosodic licenser at all levels in Bulgarian, and that, at earlier points, prosodic licensing needs to be performed by a prosodic unit other than the syllable. This unit, it will be claimed, is the mora. In order to demonstrate this, I will present a detailed analysis of the relevant phenomena in the phonology of Bulgarian. In the development of the argument I will rely on the modularity of the general framework assumed here, that of the lexical phonology and morphology.

4.2 Bulgarian 'Liquid Metathesis'

The phonological phenomenon in Bulgarian that argues for the position that the mora is a prosodic licenser is the so-called 'liquid metathesis'. A single set of derivationally and/or inflectionally related forms may exhibit 'liquid metathesis' in the following fashion (Scatton 1975:171):

(2) a. grəb 'back', grəbl'o 'hump-back', grəbnak 'back-bone'
     b. gərbove 'backs(Pl)', gərbət 'back(Def)' gərbat 'hump-backed'

(3) a. mlək 'silence!', mləkna 'be silent(Perf)', mləkvam 'be silent(Imp)'
     b. məlkom 'silently', məlčanie 'silence'

The alternating segments are a ə and a liquid, either *l* or *r*. The liquid either precedes the ə, as in (2)a and (3)a, or it follows the ə, as in (2)b and (3)b.

A remarkable fact about this alternation is that it involves only liquids, and that the only alternating vowel is ə. Furthermore, this

The Mora as a Prosodic Unit

alternation is characterizable in terms of syllable structure. The generalization proposed in Aronson 1968:147 is that given in (4):

(4)   a. /ər, əl/ occur before a heterosyllabic consonant;
       b. /rə, lə/ occur before a tautosyllabic consonant.

According to this, the syllable structure of a form like *grəbl'o* will be as in (5)a, and that of a form like *gərbat* as in (5)b.

(5)   a.

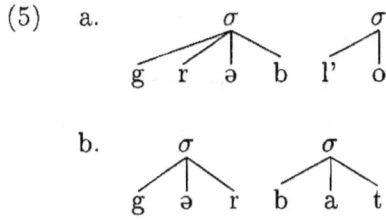

      b.
            σ   σ
         g ə r   b   a   t

However, not *all* sequences of liquid and ə participate in this alternation. There are a number of exceptions to (4), for example those listed in (6):

(6)   a. bləf 'bluff', bləfət 'bluff(Def)', bləfove 'bluff(Pl)'
       b. krəg 'circle', krəgov 'circular', krəgəl 'round'

This suggests that 'liquid metathesis' is of limited productivity, although the number of participating forms is quite substantial.

But what phonological device should we invoke to account for this alternation? A metathesis rule would be justifiable if the values of both the consonants and the vowels affected by it were unpredictable. Since this is not what we find, positing a metathesis rule would provide little insight into why this phenomenon is limited to only certain kinds of segments. A more likely account would result from positing an epenthesis rule, i.e. from the claim that the alternating vowel in (2) and (3) is not present underlyingly but gets inserted into the structure at some later point. By positing such a rule we would account more readily for the fact that only ə is found in this alternation. We would also have a natural account for the exceptions in (6): as in most other Bulgarian forms, the vowel that appears on the surface will also be present underlyingly. Since this alternation is not found with any form that has an underlying vowel, including those that have an underlying ə, the vowel in *bləf* or *krəg* will not alternate.

This line of argument has a further virtue. It opens the possibility of a more direct inquiry into why liquids are the only environment in which epenthesis operates. But before addressing this issue, we need to determine at which point in the derivation the epenthetic vowel is inserted into the structure. The evidence will come from the facts of rule ordering. In order to present those facts in sufficient detail, we will have to make a brief excursus into Bulgarian phonology.

4.3 An Excursus into Bulgarian Phonology

I will argue here that the lexical component of Bulgarian phonology contains two levels — a cyclic and a postcyclic one. Following Booij and Rubach 1987 (see also Kiparsky 1985) I assume that, in addition to the cyclic rules, there is also a class of postcyclic lexical rules which apply at the word level. Booij and Rubach propose two kinds of word domains, morphological and prosodic. I will follow here the proposal advanced in Inkelas and Zec 1988 that the word domain should be characterized in prosodic rather than in morphological terms, and will provide further arguments for this position.

In sum, I will argue that Bulgarian phonology is organized as in (7):

(7)   The organization of Bulgarian phonology:
      Level 1: Cyclic
      Level 2: Noncyclic (Domain: Phonological Word)

The evidence for the late creation of syllables comes from the interactions of the cyclic and the postcyclic levels; or more specifically, from the interaction of three lexical rules, one cyclic and two postcyclic. The cyclic rule is the rule of Yer Vocalization: Bulgarian has a pair of vowels which participate in vowel/zero alternations, known in Slavic linguistics as yers. Yers vocalize either as ə or as *e*, and in order to distinguish them from the nonalternating ə or *e*, they have commonly been assigned an abstract vocalic value. In line with this, I will assume that the yer realized as ə is underlyingly a high, back, unrounded, lax vowel, *ŭ*, and that the yer realized as *e* is underlyingly the front, high, lax vowel *ĭ*. (Yers are lax vowels, as distinct from the other Bulgarian vowels which are all tense.) The system of Bulgarian vowels, and the place of yers in it, is given in (8):

(8) i ĭ ŭ u
     e ə o
        a

I will adopt here what is known in the literature as a fairly standard formulation of the Yer Vocalization rule (see Lightner 1972, Gussman 1980, Rubach 1984, Scatton 1975):[3]

(9) Yer Vocalization (cyclic): o   o
                                  ╪ |
                                [−tense] [−tense]

The effect of this rule is illustrated in (10). Note that a yer is vocalized only if another yer follows on the next higher cycle. In (10)a only the first yer is realized, in (10)b the only yer in the form is not realized, and in (10)c two out of three yers are realized.[4]

(10) a. [[kosŭm]ŭ] ⟶ kosəm 'hair(Sg/Masc)'
     b. [[kosŭm]i] ⟶ kosmi 'hair(Pl/Masc)'
     c. [[[kosŭm]ŭ]tŭ] ⟶ kosəmət 'hair(Sg/Masc/Def)'

In (11), it is shown how this rule derives *kosəmət*, *kosəm* and *kosəmi*, operating in a cyclic fashion.

(11)			
Cycle 1	kosŭm	kosŭm	kosŭm
Yer Vocalization:	–	–	–
Cycle 2	kosŭm]ŭ	kosŭm]ŭ	kosŭm]i
Yer Vocalization:	kosəm]ŭ	kosəm]ŭ	–
Cycle 3	kosəm]ŭ]tŭ	–	–
Yer Vocalization:	kosəm]ə]tŭ	–	–
Output of Cyclic Level:	kosəmətŭ	kosəmŭ	kosŭmi

The nonvocalized yers that appear in the output forms of (11) are delinked from prosodic structure by the rule of Yer Delinking.

(12) *Yer Delinking* (postcyclic):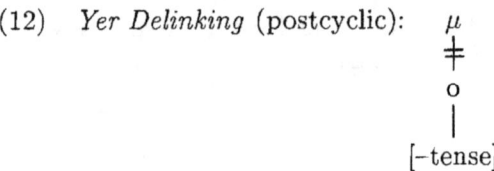

This rule will have to be postcyclic, since it cannot apply before the rule in (9) has vocalized all the yers that could be vocalized. Yet Yer Delinking is a lexical rule: I mentioned earlier that Bulgarian has a postcyclic lexical level, and it is precisely at this level that Yer Delinking applies. In particular, it applies before Final Devoicing, a postcyclic lexical rule that devoices obstruents in word final position.

(13) *Final Devoicing* (postcyclic):
C [− son] ⟶ [− voiced] / [---]$_w$

That the domain of Final Devoicing is indeed a word size domain follows from the fact that it does not apply across word boundaries. Thus, Final Devoicing applies in (14)a, where the stem *grad* 'city' is followed by a clitic, but not in (14)b, where it is followed by a suffix.

(14) a. [grad=e] ⟶ grat e '(a) city is'
b. [grad-a] ⟶ grada 'cities(QPl)'

In other words, (13) applies not on the prosodic unit formed by a clitic and its host, but on the word size unit, as given in (15):

(15) [grad]$_w$

But (15) is in the singular masculine form, whose ending is a yer vowel. Thus, before Yer Delinking applies, we have the following:

(16) [gradŭ]$_w$

Now, if Final Devoicing was ordered before Yer Delinking, it would never apply in (16), since the obstruent would not be in word final position. But with Yer Delinking ordered before Final Devoicing, we get the right result. (16) first undergoes Yer Delinking, yielding (17):

(17) [gradŭ]$_w$ ⟶ [grad]$_w$

The obstruent will now appear in word final position where it can undergo Final Devoicing.

The fact that the domain of rule application is the word does not in itself argue that this is a lexical domain. I will digress at this point to show that this domain does have a lexical status; but this becomes obvious only under the further assumption that this is also a prosodic domain. In particular, I will argue that the word size domain in question is not a morphological word but a prosodic word.[5]

One particular class of forms presents a systematic exception to the rule of Final Devoicing. According to Scatton 1984:73-74, Final Devoicing fails to apply to prepositions:

(18) a. pred mene   'before me'   (*pret mene)
      b. pod igoto   'under the yoke'   (*pot igoto)

In what follows it be will shown that this exception can be explained in a natural way only if the word size domain is taken to be prosodic.

Let us first explore the consequences of assuming that Final Devoicing operates on a morphological domain. Note that this domain should be available both lexically and postlexically, since the word is a unit both in the morphology and in the syntax. Thus, we are faced with two possibilities: Final Devoicing may apply either in the lexicon or postlexically. If it applies in the lexicon, then we have a straightforward solution: this rule will affect only those forms which, according to Kiparsky 1982a,b, undergo lexical rules, that is, the so-called content words, which comprise nouns, verbs, and adjectives, but not pronouns, auxiliaries, or prepositions. Thus, we exclude prepositions from undergoing Final Devoicing on principled grounds. But if Final Devoicing applies postlexically, there is no way of excluding prepositions as input to this rule; we would have to restrict the rule to certain lexical categories, and this is not a readily available device in the postlexical component. Thus the most likely choice in this case would be the lexical domain, unless there is a way of preventing postlexical rules from applying to prepositions. It is interesting to note that Booij and Rubach 1987, analyzing the Polish version of Final Devoicing which also fails to apply to prepositions, offer as one of the solutions to have this rule apply postlexically; prepositions are exempted from undergoing this rule due to the prior application of 'word bracket erasure', which divests prepositions of their morphological word status.

We will now examine the consequences of the other position, the one that I argue for here, that Final Devoicing applies on a prosodic domain. We can simply assume that the domain of this rule is the phonological word, formed by an algorithm in the lexical component, as proposed in Inkelas and Zec 1988. The algorithm applies in the lexicon and will therefore affect only those forms which, according to Kiparsky 1982a,b, undergo lexical rules. Since prepositions are not among those forms, they will not become phonological words, and Final Devoicing will fail to apply to them.[6]

But although phonological words are formed lexically, they may still be available postlexically; and they indeed are, given the commonly held assumptions about the inventory of prosodic units and the hierarchy they form (Hayes 1989a, Nespor and Vogel 1986). In (19) I give the relevant portion of this hierarchy:

(19) Prosodic Hierarchy (Nespor and Vogel 1986)
 phonological word
 clitic group
 phonological phrase

That is to say, although the phonological word is formed lexically, there is nothing to prevent it from being available postlexically as well, along with the clitic group. Note that Final Devoicing will not apply to prepositions postlexically either, since the only phonological words available postlexically are those formed in the lexicon. But if the domain is available both lexically and postlexically, there is no way of choosing between them on principled grounds.

To avoid problems of this sort, I propose to exclude the clitic group from the prosodic hierarchy, and to assume that the clitic group is simply the phonological word in its postlexical form. Thus, rather than assume that the phonological word and the clitic group are separate prosodic domains, we can make reference to the lexical/postlexical distinction and say that the phonological word is available only lexically; and that postlexically it automatically combines with clitics, if there are any, which potentially changes its size.[7] This gives us a revised version of the hierarchy, with no clitic group:

(20) Prosodic Hierarchy (revised version)
      phonological word
      phonological phrase

This version of the hierarchy can be further motivated. Note that the clitic group differs from the other (complex) prosodic units in that it is a combination of prosodic and nonprosodic elements — that is, of phonological words and of clitics. All the other complex units are combinations of one or more prosodic units at the immediately lower level of the hierarchy. Thus, by eliminating the clitic group from the hierarchy and opting for the version in (20), we are left with prosodic units which behave in a uniform fashion.[8]

Most importantly, this proposal eliminates certain other ambiguities that exist under the hierarchy in (19) as well. It is not clear in the literature whether phonological words are created lexically or postlexically. Furthermore, if they are created lexically, they have to be both lexical and postlexical domains. But if we eliminate clitic groups, then we get a more constrained theory. If phonological words are created lexically, we get both the lexical phonological word domain, and the larger, postlexical domain in which phonological words increase in size because they include clitics. But if phonological words are created postlexically, they come only in the larger size, that is, combined with clitics. In other words, the prediction is that, postlexically, we can never have both phonological words and clitic groups. If both domains are present in a language, one will have to be lexical and the other postlexical. As far as I can tell, there are no counterexamples to this proposal.

Let us return to Final Devoicing and its failure to apply to prepositions. We have seen that this rule applies to word size units; since phonological words come in two sizes, lexical and postlexical, Final Devoicing will have to be a lexical rule because it applies

4.4 Epenthesis

We now return to the epenthesis rule proposed in section 2. As will be seen, this rule also has to apply after the rule of Yer Delinking. Furthermore, this rule applies on the same domain as Yer Delinking and Final Devoicing: it is a postcyclic lexical rule, applying on the domain of the phonological word.

Recall that the epenthesized ə always appears before a tautosyllabic consonant. Furthermore, it can appear before at most one such consonant, since Bulgarian syllables cannot have more than one consonant in the coda. With that in mind, we can now examine how epenthesis operates on *grəb*, which is a singular masculine form, and therefore gets a yer ending. Thus, before Yer Delinking we get the form in (21):

(21) grbŭ

It will be shown that the proper surface form corresponding to (21) can be derived only if Yer Delinking is ordered before, rather than after, epenthesis. The discussion will be largely informal; epenthesis as well as syllabification will be given a more formal treatment in a later section of this chapter.

In (22), where the order is Epenthesis/Yer Delinking, the liquid and the final vowel of the stem are heterosyllabic at the point when Epenthesis applies. They become tautosyllabic later, that is after Yer Delinking, but at that point the ə has already been inserted, and we get the ill-formed *gərb:

(22) Input:

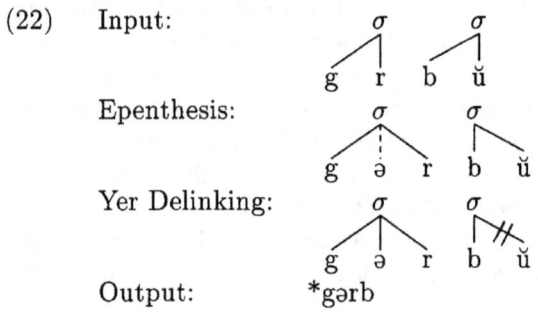

Output: *gərb

But, with Yer Delinking ordered before Epenthesis, the liquid and *b* are tautosyllabic at the point when Epenthesis applies, and we get the right result:

(23)   Input:

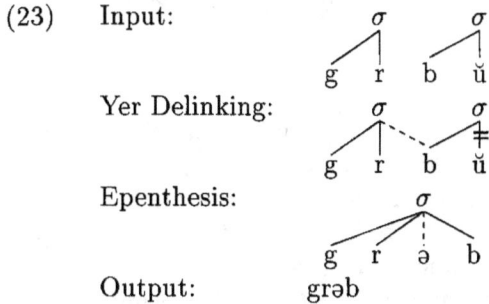

        Yer Delinking:

        Epenthesis:

        Output: grəb

But Epenthesis is also a lexical rule, since its domain of application is the word. As shown in the following examples, taken from Elson 1976, the consonant that belongs to the stem syllabifies with the vowel in the suffix (see (24)):

(24) a. grək 'Greek'
      b. gərkət '(the) Greek'
      c. gərci '(the) Greeks'

The stem-final consonant does not syllabify with the following clitic at the stage when epenthesis applies. Rather, it is treated as tautosyllabic with the preceding liquid, so that we get the syllabification as in (25)a rather than (25)b.

(25) a. grək = e
      b. *gərk = e

We have now located the point in the grammar at which the epenthesis rule applies: it applies at the postcyclic lexical level. It is crucial to point out that the word size unit relevant here is the phonological word created lexically. This unit will be available only at the lexical level; postlexically, the phonological word will incorporate clitics, and therefore be of a different size.

4.5 Formation of Prosodic Structure
4.5.1 Cyclic Domain: Moras vs. Syllables

If the vowel in a form like *grəb* is inserted by a postcyclic rule of epenthesis, the sequence found at the cyclic level is as in (26):

(26) grb

Itô's Principle of Prosodic Licensing requires that this sequence be prosodically licensed throughout the derivation, i.e. *before* the epenthesis rule applies. This will preclude stray erasure, which deletes segments that are not incorporated into prosodic structure. In other words, the sequence in (26) must be protected by prosodic structure, and we may now ask how this sequence gets prosodic licensing. Liquids are never syllabic in surface Bulgarian forms, and there is good reason to assume that they are not syllabic at the postcyclic lexical level. But are they syllabic at some earlier point? And if not, what prosodic unit is responsible for the prosodic licensing of the form in (26)?

A possible approach, one that I will argue against, might be to say that the sequence in (26) does in fact get included into syllable structure early on. In particular, we might assume that liquids are syllabic throughout the cyclic domain but not in the postcyclic domain. The possibility of liquids being syllabic is not in itself implausible. What is implausible, however, is that the syllabicity of liquids should vary from one level of lexical phonology to another. This proposal would have the undesirable consequence of imposing different, potentially conflicting, constraints on syllable structure at different lexical levels. As argued in Selkirk 1981, it would be undesirable to allow this extra power into the grammar.[9]

The alternative I will propose is that in Bulgarian syllables are not available until the postcyclic lexical level, and that at the cyclic level prosodic licensing is performed by a subsyllabic prosodic unit, namely by the mora. In what follows, I will argue that moraic structure is the only prosodic structure present through the cyclic lexical component.

The claim to be advanced here is that the set of Bulgarian moraic segments includes liquids, as shown in (27):

(27) Bulgarian moraic segments (first approximation):
liquids
vowels

Since Bulgarian liquids can be moraic, *grəb* will be assigned moraic structure as in (28):

(28)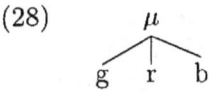

The assignment of moraic structure as in (28) follows naturally from the fact that *r* is flanked by less sonorous segments; which leaves the liquid as the only candidate for the moraic head. In this role, liquids compete only with vowels, and no vowel is present in the form under discussion.

We can now say that the form in (28) is prosodically licensed, since it is incorporated into prosodic structure. This structure is built not around syllables but around moras; if moras are prosodic units, then the moraic structure in (28) is sufficient to provide prosodic licensing.

Complex morphological forms such as *grəb* and *gərbat* illustrate the cyclic assignment of moraic structure. The basic procedure includes creation of sequences of ascending sonority, accompanied by unmorified consonant adjunction to the left, as proposed in Chapter Two.

(29) $\left[\left[\begin{array}{c}\mu\\ \wedge\\ g\ r\ b\end{array}\right]\begin{array}{c}\mu\\ |\\ \breve{u}\end{array}\right]$

(30) $\left[\left[\begin{array}{c}\mu\\ \wedge\\ g\ r\ b\end{array}\right]\begin{array}{c}\mu\\ |\\ a\end{array}\begin{array}{c}\mu\\ |\\ t\ \breve{u}\end{array}\right]$

To sum up, Bulgarian liquids are moraic segments, i.e. they are sufficiently sonorous to form moraic peaks. It now becomes clear why the vowel can be absent from the underlying structure, and why this happens only in the environment of liquids. The reason is that at the cyclic level both vowels and liquids are capable of acting as moraic peaks. Furthermore, since no syllable structure is present at that point, all moraic segments are of equal status, so that liquids and vowels pattern alike at this level. It is at the postcyclic level that differences come in, and this brings us back to the Epenthesis rule.

4.5.2 Postcyclic Lexical Domain

We have seen that Epenthesis does not apply until the postcyclic lexical level. But why does this rule become available at a relatively late point in the grammar? My claim will be that this rule is closely related to syllabification, and therefore does not enter the grammar prior to the point at which syllable structure is created.[10] In other words, the role of this rule is to 'improve' moraic structure converting it into eligible syllable structure. This proposal is in the spirit of Lapointe and Feinstein 1984 and Selkirk 1981.

The Bulgarian data presented here strongly suggest that moras are present at the early levels in the lexical phonology and that, furthermore, they are not co-present with syllables. Syllables are created at the postcyclic lexical level, by a simple mora-to-syllable mapping. This is a one-to-one mapping, since all Bulgarian syllables are monomoraic. It is important to note that the internal constituency of each mora is preserved under this mapping.

At the point at which the mora-to-syllable mapping applies, i.e. after Yer Delinking has removed yers from the structures in (28) and (30), the moraic structure of a form like *grəb* is as in (31), and that of a form like *gərbat* is as in (32):

(31)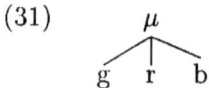

(32)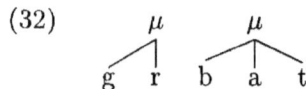

The output of the mapping is as in (33) and (34):

(33)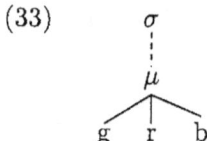

(34)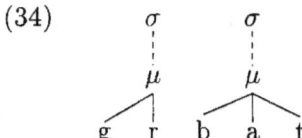

The most sonorous segment in each mora now becomes the most sonorous segment of the corresponding syllable. But as claimed earlier, a melodic segment that can serve as a moraic peak may not be able serve as a syllabic peak, since moras and syllables often posit different requirements in this respect.

Since all Bulgarian syllables are monomoraic, the single mora in the syllable will have to conform to the sonority requirements imposed by syllables. In particular, Bulgarian liquids are sufficiently sonorous to serve as proper moraic peaks, but not to serve as proper syllable peaks. Since liquids cannot act as syllable nuclei, the Epenthesis rule will insert a segment which is sonorous enough for this role.

As we have seen, it is predictable where the epenthesized vowel will appear with regard to syllable structure. Yet this does not result from a general syllable structure constraint. The maximal syllable in Bulgarian is of the CCVC type, and while the Epenthesis rule creates one possible syllable type, i.e. CVC, it does not create the other two possible types, CV or CCV.

(35)   Bulgarian syllable template: CCVC

The problem is illustrated in (36):

(36) a. grbat ⟶ gərbat (CVC)
      b. grbat ⟶ *grəbat (*CCV)
      c. grbat ⟶ *gərəbat (*CVCV)

We can explain in a straightforward manner why we do not get (36)c; deriving this form would require a disruption of moraic structure, and this will not be allowed under the mora-to-syllable mapping defined here. But although neither (36)a nor (36)b cause a disruption of moraic structure, only (36)a is well-formed. This suggests that the Epenthesis rule poses a further constraint, obligatorily creating closed syllables. The rule can be formulated as in (37) (assuming that c and v stand for consonantal and vocalic melody segments respectively):

(37)　　Epenthesis:

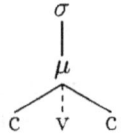

We do not need to specify in (37) that there can be at most one consonant to the right. This will follow from the general syllable structure constraint, which allows at most one consonant at the right margin.

In sum, we have examined an asymmetry in the prosodic behavior of liquids at two levels of lexical phonology. In order to account for this, I proposed that the asymmetry has its source in prosodic differences between the two levels: at one we find only moras, and at the other both moras and syllables. In fact, we would expect asymmetries like this to arise if moras and syllables obey different well-formedness constraints, and they certainly do in the case discussed here.

But although we predict asymmetry between moraic and syllabic units, certain general constraints regarding sonority will still hold. For example, while we do expect to find a moraic segment that is not syllabic, we do not expect to find a syllabic segment that is not moraic. In other words, syllabic segments will always present a subset (but not necessarily a proper subset) of moraic segments in any given language, as argued in Chapter One.

4.5.3 Apparent Counterexamples

There are two classes of exceptions to the analysis presented here. The first class are forms derived by some (although not all) suffixes which begin with a yer vowel. The stem *vrh*, for example, obtains the epenthetic vowel in the regular fashion in all forms other than those combined with the suffix *-ĭn*:

(38)　vrəh 'top' *vs.* vərhət 'top(Def.)'

(39)　vrəhen *vs.* vrəhna

That this behavior is not found with all yer suffixes is shown by the regular alternation triggered by the suffix *ic̆*:

(40) gərnec *vs.* grənca

I will propose that, in certain cases, the rule of Yer Delinking applies at the cyclic level as well, and that this application is triggered by a specific set of suffixes. This process is illustrated in (41):

(41) Yer Delinking:

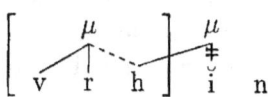

The 'onset' consonant will delink to the left, creating a form which is input to the Epenthesis Rule, which will apply as in (42):

(42) Epenthesis:

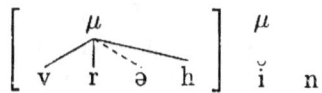

This account gains in plausibility given the fact that in Serbo-Croatian, a language closely related to Bulgarian, we also find Yer Delinking applying at the cyclic levels, as will be shown in Chapter Five. Furthermore, this rule again affects only a subclass of yer suffixes.[11] In Bulgarian the yer suffixes which undergo Yer Delinking exhibit idiosyncracies with respect to the Epenthesis Rule; in Serbo-Croatian the idiosyncratic properties of such suffixes are that they trigger compensatory lengthening (see 5.3), and fail to be linked to tone (see 5.8). In both cases the idiosyncracies are readily explainable in terms of Yer Delinking.

The second class of exceptions are the nominative singular forms as in (43):

(43) dəlg 'debt' *vs.* dəlgət 'debt (Def.)'

The Epenthesis Rule proposed here would generate *dləg, on a par with grəb or vrəh. Furthermore, the well-formed dəlg does not conform to the Bulgarian syllable template in (35), since it creates a CVCC syllable. An obvious solution seems to be positing the extrametricality of the stem final consonant. In this case, consonant extrametricality would be assigned by rule, which would have to apply postcyclically, after the application of Yer Delinking; this rule would affect only a class of specially marked forms.

4.6 Further Implications

It has been demonstrated that we need to distinguish between syllabic and moraic segments not only in syntagmatic terms, i.e. within syllable structure, but also across different levels. Thus, although Bulgarian does not distinguish between light and heavy syllables, we still find a distinction between moraic and syllabic segments. In particular, moraic segments in Bulgarian occupy the portion of the sonority hierarchy given in (44):

(44) Bulgarian moraic segments:
liquids
vowels

We now need to address the further issue of which among the Bulgarian moraic segments are also syllabic. Or, to phrase it differently, are all segments that are more sonorous than liquids syllabic in Bulgarian?

The behavior of yers suggests that this may not be the case. In particular, we might have an account for the fall of yers if we assume that, like liquids, yers are moraic but not syllabic. This will give us a more elaborate sonority hierarchy, specifically that in (45), as well as the set of syllabic segments which excludes high lax vowels, i.e. yers.

(45) Bulgarian syllabic and moraic segments:
obstruents
nasals
liquids
high lax vowels
remaining vowels

Moras headed with yers will then fail to be included into syllable structure (unless the yers have previously undergone lowering, of course). For example, the form in (46) will be syllabified as follows:

(46)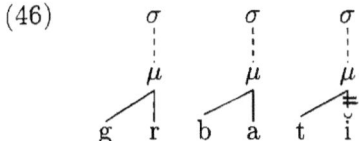

The final mora will fail to form a properly headed syllable because the yer sound it contains is not sufficiently sonorous to act as syllable peak. Since no repair mechanism will come to its rescue, this mora fails to be incorporated into higher prosodic structure, and eventually undergoes stray erasure.[12]

Thus although sonority requirements are placed on every single mora, they are identical only in the absence of syllable structure. If moras are incorporated into syllables, sonority requirements on an individual mora will depend on its position within syllable structure.

This explains why in languages that have only monomoraic syllables the sets of moraic and syllabic segments are identical on the surface: the distinction between moraic and syllabic segments becomes neutralized due to the fact that all moras bear the s label. But these may still be distinct sets, as is the case in Bulgarian, and this could be signaled by various discrepancies in the behavior of segments at different levels.

Furthermore, the kinds of asymmetry that exist between different levels in Bulgarian are precisely those that exist within a bimoraic syllable. Languages which possess bimoraic syllables in addition to the monomoraic ones allow greater diversity of patterns since their moras can bear either the s or the w label. Recall that our framework makes a number of predictions about the distribution of moraic and syllabic segments. In particular, we expect that the moraic r would not trigger epenthesis when occupying the w position. Of course, this prediction can be tested only on languages with bimoraic syllables, and Bulgarian is not such a language.

4.7 Implications for Prosodic Phonology

I have argued here for including moras into the prosodic hierarchy, that is for the version of the hierarchy as in (47):

(47) Prosodic Hierarchy
phonological phrase
phonological word
foot
syllable
mora

As I mentioned at the beginning of this chapter, it is generally assumed that the syllable is the lowest unit of prosodic hierarchy (see McCarthy and Prince 1986, Selkirk 1978, Nespor and Vogel 1986). But I have argued here for a *subsyllabic* prosodic level. My claim is that moraic structure constitutes an appropriate level of subsyllabic prosodic units. Furthermore, if we make moras prosodic units, then from a few well known principles we derive certain predictions about moraic behavior.

Let me go back to Itô's 1986 principle of Prosodic Licensing, repeated in (48):

(48) *Prosodic Licensing:* Phonological units have to be incorporated into (higher) prosodic structure (modulo extraprosodicity). [Itô 1986]

The principle in (48) has a dual function: it requires both that nonprosodic units be incorporated into prosodic structure, and that lower prosodic units be included into higher ones. As mentioned earlier, elements that are left out of prosodic structure will be subject to stray erasure, and thus incapable of ever appearing on the surface.

If the mora is a prosodic unit, it will have to satisfy both of these conditions. First, it should be able to provide prosodic licensing of nonprosodic phonological units; this role can be performed by moras, as demonstrated in the case of Bulgarian. And second, it should be part of higher prosodic structure — a requirement which is met if the syllable is represented as in (46) and (47), i.e. as consisting of moras. In particular, Selkirk's 1984b:26 Strict Layer Hypothesis, which in a sense complements the principle in (48), specifies in what manner levels of prosodic structure should be incorporated into one another:

(49) *Strict Layer Hypothesis:* A category of level i in the hierarchy immediately dominates (a sequence of) categories at level $i - 1$. [Selkirk 1984b]

If we set the value *1* for moras, it follows from (49) that moras are incorporated into syllables, which are units at the next higher level. And the representation of syllable internal structure as in (50) follows directly from this.

(50)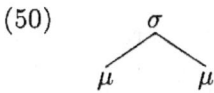

Furthermore, if the co-presence of moras and syllables is not necessary, that is if we can find levels of representation with only one but not the other of these units present, then the theory of prosodic phonology makes clear predictions as to what situations are to be expected. In particular, given the Strict Layer Hypothesis, we expect to find levels with moras but no syllables present; but we do not expect to find levels with syllables but no moras present.

Notes

[1] Parts of this chapter appear in Zec 1988.

[2] Itô 1989 at least implicitly claims that moras can provide prosodic licensing, by having syllabification apply on morified structure.

[3] There have been attempts at formulating this rule in an autosegmental framework (see Kenstowicz and Rubach 1987 for Slovak) but I will continue assuming that this rule applies at the melody tier.

[4] The example listed in (51)c contains the definite article in the masculine singular form, -tŭ. There is a controversy in the Slavic literature as to whether the definite article in Bulgarian should be classified as a suffix or as a clitic (see Elson 1976 and the references therein). Note that the yer in the article triggers the vocalization of the yer in the singular masculine ending. This should be taken as indisputable evidence that the article is a suffix rather than a clitic, since only suffixes can undergo cyclic rules.

[5] My position thus differs from that of Booij and Rubach 1987, where it is assumed that postcyclic rules have at their disposal both morphological and prosodic domains.

[6] However, not all phonological words are created lexically. In languages like English, prepositions, for example, obtain the phonological word status postlexically, as claimed in Zec and Inkelas 1987. Note that this class of words cannot become phonological word by virtue of a lexical algorithm because they do not undergo lexical rules.

[7] Here I follow Inkelas 1987, 1989 in assuming that clitics are included into one of the prosodic domains by virtue of their prosodic subcategorization frames.

[8] As shown in Inkelas 1988b, the Hausa clitic *fa* subcategorizes for the phonological phrase. By retaining the clitic group within the prosodic hierarchy, we run into the paradox of having the clitic group both below and above the phonological phrase, which presents another important argument for excluding the clitic group from the hierarchy.

[9] An analysis in terms of degenerate syllables along the lines of Selkirk 1981, according to which syllables can have unfilled nuclei, would run into the same problems as the insertion of a ə prior to Yer Delinking (potentially at the cyclic level). The position of the unfilled nucleus before Yer Delinking would not necessarily

correspond to its position after Yer Delinking. In other words, there would be no crucial difference between an analysis which posits degenerate syllables, and an analysis which inserts ə, at any point in the derivation prior to Yer Delinking. See also Lapointe and Feinstein 1984 on this point.

[10] One of the principles of Lexical Phonology (Kiparsky 1984, 1985) is the Strong Domain Hypothesis, which says that rules enter the grammar at the lowest level, unless conditioned by something that comes in later. Here, epenthesis is related to syllable structure, and will not be able to enter the grammar before syllable structure is created. Therefore, this proposal is not at odds with the Strong Domain Hypothesis.

[11] The difference between the two classes of suffixes in Serbo-Croatian is expressed in terms of level ordering. I have not explored the issue of positing more than one cyclic level in Bulgarian, and at this point the difference between the two classes of suffixes is marked diacritically.

[12] The question arises why in this case we have stray erasure rather than, say, epenthesis, as a repair mechanism. One reason might be that Bulgarian does not have diphthongs, and any epenthesis process that inserts a vowel next to a yer would create a segment of this kind.

5

Case Study: Serbo-Croatian

5.1 Introduction

The goal of this chapter is to supply further evidence for the prosodic status of the mora and, more generally, for the relative independence of moraic and syllabic structure. It will be shown that, just like Bulgarian, Serbo-Croatian also has moras but lacks syllables at the earliest lexical level, while later levels contain both moras and syllables. However, the range of phenomena that manifest this organization is very different from that in Bulgarian. The phonological phenomena in Serbo-Croatian that will provide crucial arguments for the prosodic status of the mora are certain lengthening processes and the system of accent assignment. The sources of the data are Belić 1956, Daničić 1925, Leskien 1914, 1975, Matešić 1970, and Nikolić 1970.

We will first examine the organization of the Serbo-Croatian phonology. The lexical component contains three levels, two cyclic and one postcyclic, as shown in (1). The two cyclic levels are characterized both by the morphological and by the phonological operations that apply on them, while the postcyclic level is further characterized in prosodic terms: phonological and morphological processes applying at this level operate on the prosodic domain of the phonological word.

(1) Level One: Compounding, Derivation (cyclic)
Level Two: Derivation, Inflection (cyclic)
Level Three: —   (noncyclic; domain: phonological word)

Given this partitioning into levels, it will be shown that Level

One contains only moras but no syllables; and that the higher levels contain both types of prosodic units. We then discuss two phonological processes that strongly argue for this position: one that operates at Level One and requires presence of moras but absence of syllables; and one that operates at Level Two, and makes crucial reference to syllable structure. The first process is the so-called presonorant lengthening, and the second one is accent assignment.

The proposal that accent assignment starts applying at Level Two calls for an explicit statement about how rules are distributed across levels. A highly constrained view of this is expressed by the Strong Domain Hypothesis (Kiparsky 1984). According to this hypothesis

> all rules are potentially applicable at the first level of the lexicon, and apply there provided only that the principles of grammar permit it; at lower levels of the lexicon and in the postlexical phonology rules may be "turned off" but no new ones may be added. [Kiparsky 1984:142]

It may appear that having the rule of accent assignment apply at Level Two is at odds with the Strong Domain Hypothesis. Note however that we can motivate a later application of this rule on independent grounds, thus making its absence at Level One compatible with the Strong Domain Hypothesis: accent assignment operates on syllables, and syllables are not available at Level One. This then naturally defers the application of this rule until a later level. Even though the rule itself may be available through Level One, its domain of application will be unavailable, which makes the application of this rule impossible.[1]

Before turning to the details of the Serbo-Croatian phonology, we need to comment on the processes of morification and syllabification. Serbo-Croatian syllables are formed very much like in Bulgarian: mora to syllable mapping is one-to-one. The only difference is that, unlike Bulgarian, Serbo-Croatian has long vowels specified underlyingly. The question arises whether the algorithm assigns the two moras linked to the same segment to different syllables. In fact, I will claim that this never happens, that is, that the syllabification algorithm cannot create a situation as in (2):

(2)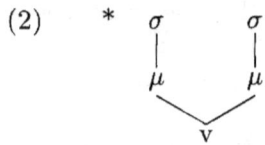

In other words, a doubly linked vowel cannot be 'split' by syllabification; its two moras have to be assigned to the same syllable.[2] This explains why Serbo-Croatian has syllables with long vowels, but none with diphthongs (see Lehiste and Ivić 1967). Since the syllabification algorithm operates in a one-to-one fashion, the two parts of a diphthong will have to be assigned to different syllables.

The set of Serbo-Croatian syllabic segments is as in (3); all these segments, including the syllabic liquid, can be doubly linked.

(3) Serbo-Croatian syllabic segments:
r
vowels

The facts of presonorant lengthening to be examined in the next section strongly suggest that sonorants and vowels may be the only moraic segments in Serbo-Croatian, and this is what I will hypothesize at this point. Note that the Serbo-Croatian v patterns with sonorants (Belić 1956:55).

(4) Serbo-Croatian moraic segments:
v
nasals
liquids
vowels

The lists of syllabic and moraic segments in (3) and (4) make Serbo-Croatian a Type Three language: the set of syllabic segments is a proper subset of the moraic one, which in turn is a proper subset of the segment inventory. However, due to the syllabification algorithm of a highly constrained type, moraic segments will never contribute to weight unless they also happen to be syllabic, and doubly linked. Thus, sonorants will play a very different role at those levels at which only moras are present, and at those at which syllables are present as well.

We now turn to the two processes that argue for this specific

Case Study: Serbo-Croatian 115

arrangement of prosodic constituents. Sections 5.2–5.3 focus on presonorant lengthening and the related phenomena, while sections 5.4–5.9 focus on tone linking.

5.2 Presonorant Lengthening

In this section I argue that only moras are operative at Level One. The phenomenon that demonstrates this is the process of presonorant lengthening, which applies cyclically, at Level One.[3] Assuming that syllabification does not operate until Level Two, and that it operates in cyclic fashion, will account for the fact that presonorant lengthening applies at Level One, but not at Level Two.

In subsection 5.2.1 I focus on a special class of vowels, the so-called yers, which play an important role in this lengthening process. The facts about presonorant lengthening, together with a moraic analysis of these facts, are presented in subsection 5.2.2.

5.2.1 Yer Vowels

Since the yer vowels, or rather, the suffixes that contain them, play an important role in the present discussion, we need to look at the place of these vowels in the phonology of Serbo-Croatian.

As we saw in Chapter Four, in the analysis of Bulgarian, yers are a class of abstract vowels realized phonetically under a specific set of conditions: a yer vowel is vocalized when followed by another yer. This accounts for the alternation in (5), where a yer (represented as ă) is realized as *a* when followed by another yer, but remains unrealized when this is not the case.

(5) a. săn-ă 'dream-Nom/Sg' → *san*
     b. săn-a 'dream-Gen/Sg' → *sna*

The rules responsible for this are Yer Vocalization and Yer Delinking. Yer Vocalization is a cyclic rule which applies both at Level One and at Level Two. The cyclicity of this rule is illustrated in (6), where the stem *săn* combines with the diminutive suffix *-ăk*, which also contains a yer:

(6) a. săn-ăk-ă 'dream(diminutive)-Nom/Sg' → *sanak*
     b. săn-ăk-a 'dream(diminutive)-Gen/Sg' → *sanka*

In order to formulate this rule, we will need to focus on the representation of yers. Yers in Serbo-Croatian surface as *a*. It has been claimed in Halle 1979 that this single vowel quality does not account for the fact that certain suffixes which begin in a yer vowel palatalize the preceding consonant (e.g. -ăsk, as in *junak* vs. *junački* or *monah* vs. *monaški*), while other suffixes beginning in a yer fail to do so. For example, the yer of the nominative singular masculine desinence does not cause palatalization (e.g. *junak-ă* becomes *junak*). This has been taken as evidence that there are two yer vowels, one front and the other back, and that only the former triggers palatalization. This analysis has been modeled on those proposed for other Slavic languages, where the palatalizing and the nonpalatalizing yers are realized as a front and a back vowel respectively. One way of accounting for the difference between Serbo-Croatian and the other Slavic languages might be to say that the underlying contrast became neutralized in Serbo-Croatian, and this is precisely what is proposed in Halle 1979.[4]

However, it will be sufficient to posit a single yer vowel underlyingly. Serbo-Croatian has five other vowels:[5]

(7)   i   u
      e   o
      a

I propose to place *a* among the front vowels, on the basis of the palatalization pattern. In addition to *e* and *i*, the vowel *a* triggers palatalization as well, which suggests that the three vowels form a natural class. My claim will be that what they have in common is the feature [−back].

Palatalization is not an automatic rule in Serbo-Croatian, or at least not when triggered by *e* and *a*.[6] While palatalization is triggered only by suffixes which begin with *i*, *e* or *a*, it is not the case that all such suffixes trigger palatalization. In (8)-(9), we see pairs of suffixes beginning with *e* and *a* respectively; the first suffix in each pair triggers palatalization while the second does not.

(8)   a. -an: sunc-e 'sun' *vs.* sunč-an 'sunny'
      b. -a: ruuk-a 'hand Nom/Sg'

(9)   a. -e: ludaač-e 'lunatic Voc/Sg'
      b. -e: ludaak-e 'lunatic Acc/Pl'

Case Study: Serbo-Croatian

From this we can conclude that palatalization is triggered only by front vowels, and that *a* needs to be represented as in (10); the feature [+tense] will be associated with all Serbo-Croatian vowels other than the yer.

(10) /a/:   [+low, –high, –back, +tense]

More generally, we can say that palatalization is governed both phonologically and morphologically. Phonologically, it simply consists in spreading the feature [–back]. But this rule will apply only if the suffixes that satisfy the phonological condition are also morphologically marked as rule triggers.[7]

Returning to yers, note that they exhibit this same pattern: some but not all suffixes beginning in this vowel trigger palatalization. This suggests that the yer is also a front vowel, and I will in fact propose that it minimally differs from *a* in being lax; all the other vowels, including *a*, will be tense. The feature matrix for yer is given in (11):

(11) /ă/:   [+low, –high, –back, –tense]

In view of this, the Serbo-Croatian vowel system has to be represented as in (12), with two back and four front vowels:

(12)

i	u
e	o
a ă	

In conclusion, there is no need to postulate two different yer vowels in order to account for the palatalization facts. Whatever accounts for the distinction between palatalizing and nonpalatalizing suffixes containing *a* or *e* will also account for the distinction between palatalizing and nonpalatalizing yers.

Yer Vocalization can then be formulated as shown in (13), where the tenseness feature is delinked from the root node.[8] And, since yer is taken to be the only lax vowel in Serbo-Croatian, loss of this feature automatically alters its vowel quality.

(13) Yer Vocalization: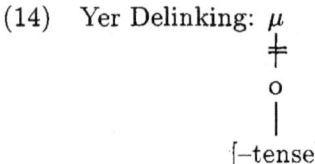

Once the feature [−tense] is delinked, this segment will share all its features with a; it will get the specification [+tense] by (postlexical) default rules.

The other rule responsible for the yer facts, Yer Delinking, is a cyclic rule which delinks a yer from its mora, as shown in (14).

(14) Yer Delinking: μ
$$\neq$$
o
|
[−tense]

This rule will eventually delete all unvocalized yers, operating at Level Three, after Yer Vocalization has been turned off. However, Yer Delinking applies at the earlier levels as well. We will come back to this in the following subsection.

5.2.2 The Conditioning Environment

A vowel is lengthened before a stem-final sonorant if followed by certain suffixes beginning in a yer vowel, although not by all such suffixes (Leskien 1975). Given this, we might in fact assume that the presence of a yer is part of the structural description of this process. At present, let us adopt the formulation of presonorant lengthening in (15); later in this section I offer an alternative analysis.

(15) $\left[\begin{array}{ccc} \ldots & [-\text{cons}] & [+\text{cons}, +\text{son}] \\ \mu & \mu & \end{array} \right]$ ă

Below is given a list of suffixes which trigger the rule in (15), together with the relevant examples. The examples include stems ending in a sonorant, where the lengthening takes place, and those ending in an obstruent, where no lengthening occurs. As noted in the introductory part of this chapter, the consonant v patterns with sonorants in Serbo-Croatian.

Case Study: Serbo-Croatian

We will start with the adjective forming suffix -ăn; the forms with sonorants are listed in (16), and those with obstruents in (17).[9]

(16) a. sila 'power' vs. siilan 'powerful'
 b. slava 'fame' vs. slaavan 'famous'
 c. otrov 'poison' vs. otroovan 'poisonous'
 d. olovo 'lead, plumb' vs. oloovan 'leaden'
 e. odmor 'rest' vs. odmooran 'rested'
 f. vera 'faith' vs. veeran 'faithful'

(17) a. rat 'war' vs. ratni 'pertaining to war'
 b. čudo 'oddity' vs. čudan 'strange'
 c. jad 'misery' vs. jadan 'miserable'

Next, we will look at the diminutive suffix -ăk which forms feminine nouns; (18) lists forms with sonorants, and (19) those with obstruents.

(18) a. sen 'shadow' vs. seenka
 b. žena 'woman' vs. žeenka
 c. maslina 'olive' vs. masliinka
 d. slama 'straw' vs. slaamka
 e. troje 'a group of three' vs. troojka 'a group of three'

(19) a. voće 'fruit' vs. voćka
 b. prah 'powder' vs. praška

Finally, we will consider the noun-forming suffixes -ăstv, illustrated in (20) and (21), and -ăc, illustrated in (22) and (23).

(20) a. troje 'three' 'vs. troojstvo 'trinity'
 b. izdaja 'treason' vs. izdaajstvo 'treachery'
 c. lukav 'sly' vs. lukaavstvo
 d. pijan 'drunk' vs. pijaanstvo

(21) a. brat 'brother' vs. bratstvo
 b. rob 'slave' vs. ropstvo

(22) a. loviti 'hunt' *vs.* loovac 'hunter'
 b. pevati 'sing' *vs.* peevac 'rooster'
 c. tvoriti 'create' *vs.* tvoorac 'creator'
 d. boriti (se) 'fight' *vs.* boorac 'fighter'

(23) a. kositi 'mow' *vs.* kosac 'mower'
 b. prositi 'beg' *vs.* prosac 'suitor'

As already mentioned, in addition to these there are also certain yer suffixes which do not trigger presonorant lengthening. Below are listed cases with the adjective forming suffix -*ăsk* and the nominative singular masculine ending -*ă*:

(24) a. jezer-o 'lake' *vs.* jezerski
 b. polj-e 'field' *vs.* poljski
 c. starin-a 'antiquity' *vs.* starinski
 d. konj 'horse' *vs.* konjski

(25) a. konj-ă → konj 'horse'
 b. zmaj-ă → zmaj 'dragon'
 c. lom-ă → lom 'disorder'

One way of distinguishing between those yer suffixes that trigger the rule in (15) and those that do not might be to mark the latter class as exceptional to this rule. However, I will propose an alternative account of these facts which makes use of the independently motivated level ordering. We will assume that presonorant lengthening operates at Level One, and that the suffixes which fail to trigger this rule belong to Level Two.

(26)

Level One	ăn	ăstv	ăk	ăc
Level Two	ăsk	ă		

This distribution over levels is supported by two independent sets of facts: by the relative ordering of the two classes of suffixes, and by the facts of tone linking.

The relative ordering of the two classes of yer suffixes is fully consistent with the distribution of their distribution across levels given in (26). The situation with the nominative singular mas-

Case Study: Serbo-Croatian

culine ending -ă is straightforward. All inflectional suffixes follow the derivational ones in Serbo-Croatian, and this is also true of the nominative singular ending, which regularly appears at the outermost cycle. Thus, this suffix is always ordered after the derivational suffixes, including those that begin with a yer.

That the suffix -ăsk, a derivational suffix which fails to trigger presonorant lengthening, is ordered after those that do trigger this rule can be demonstrated by inspecting the derived form *dostojanstvenički* 'pertaining to dignitary'. This rule is derived by six cycles of derivation, as shown in (27):

(27) a. dostoj-ăn
 b. dostoj-ăn-ăstv
 c. dostoj-ăn-ăstv-en
 d. dostoj-ăn-ăstv-en-ik
 e. dostoj-ăn-ăstv-en-ik-ăsk
 f. dostoj-ăn-ăstv-en-ik-ăsk-i → dostojanstvenički

Note that -ăsk, added at the cycle of (27)e, appears outside two of the four suffixes that trigger presonorant lengthening, -ăn and -ăstv; -ăn is introduced in (27)a, and -ăstv in (27)d.

Furthermore, -ăsk also comes after -ăc, as shown in (28):

(28) a. lov-ăc
 b. lov-ăc-ăsk
 c. lov-ăc-ăsk-i → lovački

I have found no cases of -ăk cooccurring with the suffix -ăsk; however, the suffix -ăk commonly appears very close to the stem, and it is reasonable to assume that no conflict is likely to arise here.

Further evidence for placing the suffixes -ăsk and -ă at Level Two comes from the process of tone linking, as will be argued in section 5.8.

5.3 The Analysis

As we saw, the rule of presonorant lengthening is triggered by sonorants but not by obstruents. We get a natural account of this process under the assumption that only sonorants are moraic, as suggested in the introductory part of this chapter.

I propose to replace presonorant lengthening in (15), by the rule of Yer Delinking (in (14)), which is independently motivated in the grammar. The rule is repeated in (29):

(29) Yer Delinking (cyclic):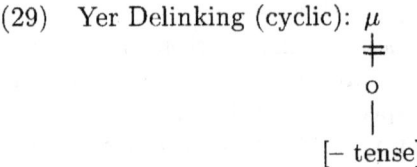

In virtue of strict cyclicity, (29) will delink those yers that appear in a suffix, but not those in roots.[10] The lengthening process will then be accounted for in terms of compensatory lengthening: the mora that comes from the delinked yer will link to a preceding vowel.[11]

To show how (29) operates at Level One, we give in (30) the derivation of two forms, one ending in an obstruent and one ending in a sonorant. The rules that apply on Cycle One are, first, Morification and, second, Yer Delinking. After the yer gets delinked, its mora remains linked to the 'onset' consonant. If the consonant is an obstruent, it will delink from the mora and adjoin to the left. And, if the consonant is a sonorant, the mora can remain since, being moraic, this consonant is capable of licensing it.

(30) *Morification* :

 YerDelinking :

 Adjunction :

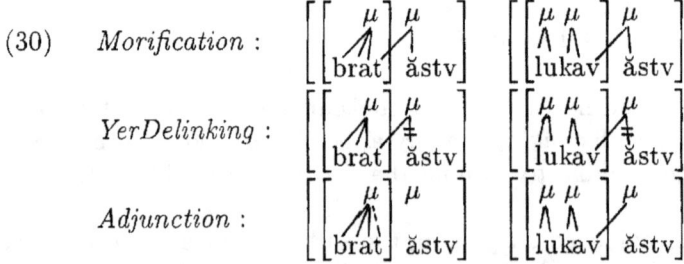

What is essential is that, at the end of the cycle, the sonorant is linked to its own mora, while the obstruent is adjoined to the left. The actual lengthening occurs at a later point, when moras are grouped into syllables, and this brings us to Level Two, where syllabification first applies.

Recall that mora to syllable mapping operates in a one-to-one fashion. Given this, the two forms in (30) undergo syllabification as in (31):

(31)   *Syllabification*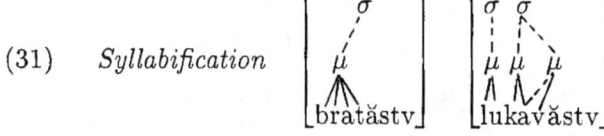

Moras will be mapped into syllables only if their heads also belong to the syllabic set, since Serbo-Croatian has no repair mechanisms at its disposal. Thus, the mora headed by v will not be mapped into a syllable, and will have to be licensed by the preceding syllable. But this will be possible only if the head vowel of the preceding syllable spreads to the unsyllabifiable mora, as shown in (31).

An important property of cyclic presonorant lengthening is that it is triggered both by those yers that are vocalized and by those that are not, as illustrated in (32)-(33):

(32)   a. slav-ăn-ă → slaavan
       b. slav-ăn-a → slaavna

(33)   a. sil-ăn-ă → siilan
       b. sil-ăn-a → siilna

The cyclic rule of Yer Delinking operates on a lower cycle than Yer Vocalization, which prevents it from distinguishing between vocalized and unvocalized yers.

At Level Two, where the morification and the syllabification algorithms operate hand in hand, a segment will be capable of heading a mora only if it can also head the corresponding syllable. In other words, those moraic segments that are not syllabic will not have a chance of preserving the moraic status. Thus, if we take two forms that combine with a Level Two suffix beginning in a yer, as in (34), no lengthening will take place.

(34) Syllabification :

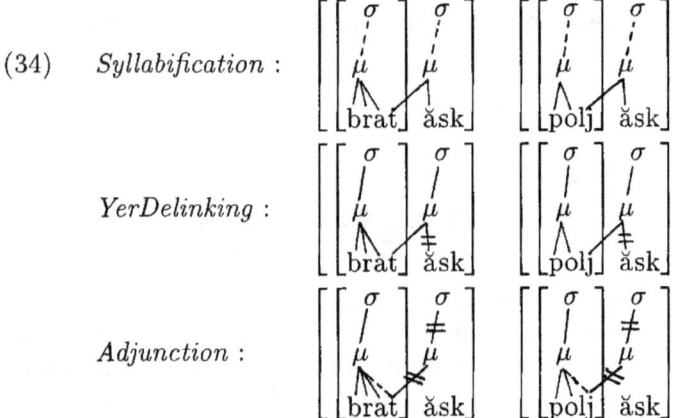

Note that both the obstruent and the sonorant are adjoined to the left; this is because the mora that the yer is delinked from is linked to a syllable node. In particular, the sonorant *lj* cannot license a mora because this mora is also linked to the syllable and can be licensed only by those segments that can also license syllables. In the derivation in (30), which takes place at Level One where no syllables are present, the sonorant is capable of licensing a mora, which subsequently causes the compensatory lengthening of the preceding vowel, as we saw in (31). Thus, although sonorants are moraic, this information will be lost at Level Two due to the restricted inventory of syllable types.

There is additional evidence that moras are independent of syllable structure at Level One but not at Level Two. Some of the Level One suffixes impose templatic constraints which are statable in terms of moras, and in some cases unstatable in terms of syllables.[12] We will examine four such suffixes: *-at*, *-ăk*, the comparative ending *-i* and the plural augment *-ov/-ev*.

Let us first look at *-at*. In (35) we see that the long vowel of the stem is shortened before *-at*, and that all stems this suffix attaches to are monosyllabic.

(35) a. brk- 'moustache' — brk-at
       a. nos- 'nose' — nos-at
       b. krošnj- 'foliage' — krošnj-at
       c. kriil- 'wing' — kril-at
       d. glaav- 'head' — glav-at
       e. graan- 'branch' — gran-at

Case Study: Serbo-Croatian

This suggests that the template of the suffix -*at* requires a degenerate moraic foot. Moreover, the suffix -*i* attaches to forms under the same condition, that is, only if they consist of a non-branching moraic foot; and shortening is again a 'repair mechanism', as shown in (36):[13]

(36) a. brz- 'fast' — brži
      b. dug- 'long' — duži
      c. žuut- 'yellow' — žući
      d. plaav- 'blue' — plavlji
      e. crrn- 'black' — crnji
      f. kriiv- 'crooked' — krivlji
      g. suuv- 'dry' — suvlji

Furthermore, disyllabic forms like those in (37) seem to be reduced to monosyllables by the same process:

(37) a. kratak- 'short' — kraći
      b. dubok- 'long' — dublji
      c. nizak- 'low' — niži
      d. visok- 'tall' — viši

The above forms end in adjective-forming suffixes -*ăk* and -*ok*; these suffixes are added to roots unspecified for category, to convert them into adjectives (other suffixes are added to convert those roots into other categories). We can either assume that *i* attaches directly to the root, before it gets any category specification; or that it is added after the attachment of the adjective-forming suffix, and that the same shortening process that we saw in (37) applies here as well. Note that a 'syllable with a long vowel' corresponds to a branching moraic foot just like 'two short syllables', as is the case in (37); in one case the degenerate foot is formed by means of vowel shortening, and in the other, by the loss of the 'second syllable'.

Finally, the plural augment -*ov* also exhibits templatic properties; in this case, the condition appears to be that the form this augment attaches to has to be a moraic foot, branching or non-branching. This is the only characterization that can account for the fact that this form attaches to monosyllables with either a short or a long vowel, as in (38) and (39) respectively, and to disyllabic forms in which both syllables are short, as in (40):

(38) a. rok — rokovi 'timespan'
 b. ded — dedovi 'grandfather'
 c. kuk — kukovi 'hip'

(39) a. liik — liikovi 'image'
 b. kraalj — kraaljevi 'king'
 c. kljuuč — kljuučevi 'key'

(40) a. jablan — jablanovi 'poplar'
 b. vitez — vitezovi 'knight'

Level Two suffixes do not exhibit templatic properties; they can affect the vowel length of the stem final syllable, but never the moraic foot structure of the entire stem.

We will now turn to the rule of accent assignment, which operates at Level Two. As will be shown, this rule requires the presence of syllables in the prosodic structure.

5.4 The Accentual System

5.4.1 Background Information

Serbo-Croatian is traditionally viewed as having four pitch accents, whose distribution is largely unpredictable (see Lehiste and Ivić 1986 and the references therein). Examples of the four accentual types are given in (41):

(41) a. Short Falling: šŭma 'forest'
 b. Long Falling: zâstava 'flag'
 c. Short Rising: màlina 'raspberry'
 d. Long Rising: rázlika 'difference'

The traditional characterization contains three redundancies (Browne and McCawley 1965, Jakobson 1962, Halle 1971). First, the difference between the long and the short accents is reducible to the difference in vowel length. Second, while the rising accents can appear on any syllable of a polysyllabic word, with the exception of the final one, the falling accents can appear only on the initial syllable. And third, the falling accents reside within a single syllable, while the rising accents stretch over two syllables.

Most of these redundancies have been eliminated in the analysis of Browne and McCawley 1965, which associates one syllable in the word with an accent diacritic. If the diacritically marked syllable is noninitial, then the immediately preceding syllable is interpreted as having special prosodic status as well. This derives the difference between the falling accents, that is, those that are initial, and the rising ones, that is, those that are not initial. This approach also derives the monosyllabic nature of the falling accents and the disyllabic nature of the rising ones. However, under this approach no predictions are made about the prosodic properties of the syllable associated with the diacritic, or the one immediately preceding it.

A further step towards delimiting what is predictable in the Serbo-Croatian accentual system is made in Inkelas and Zec 1988. As Lehiste and Ivić show, the Serbo-Croatian accent has two relevant phonetic correlates — pitch and duration. Taking duration to be a correlate of stress, and pitch a correlate of tone, Inkelas and Zec decompose accent into tone and stress, and then show that the occurrence of stress is predictable from tone, although the occurrence of tone is not predictable from stress. Surface pitch properties of the words listed in (41) can be represented as in (42):

(42)   a. Short Falling: šȕma šuma

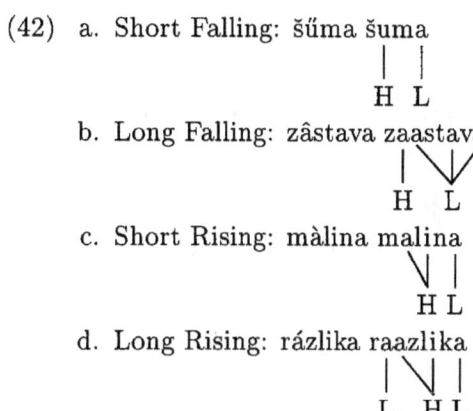

b. Long Falling: zâstava zaastava

c. Short Rising: màlina malina

d. Long Rising: rázlika raazlika

Given the tonal array in (42), it is possible to predict the occurrence of stress, which appears on the leftmost syllable linked to a High. But this representation makes certain other correct predictions as well. Recall that Serbo-Croatian bimoraic syllables contain long vowels. If we assume that the mora is a tone-bearing unit, and if the mapping of tones to tone-bearing units is one-to-one, then it follows naturally that contours will appear only on syllables with long vowels: (42)b and (42)d have HL and LH contours on their initial syllables respectively.

Inkelas and Zec propose to derive the surface forms in (42) from the underlying forms as in (43). The essential move is to assume that only High tones are present lexically (by appealing to underspecification), while Low tones are introduced postlexically. This gives us the lexical representations as in (43):

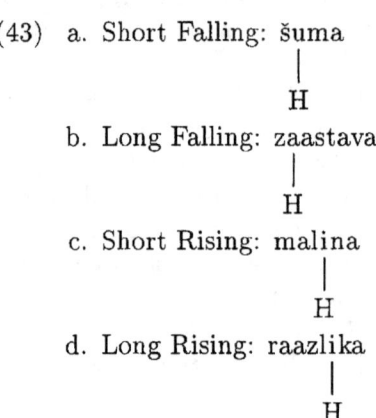

(43) a. Short Falling: šuma
            |
            H
     b. Long Falling: zaastava
            |
            H
     c. Short Rising: malina
            |
            H
     d. Long Rising: raazlika
            |
            H

It is further assumed that the rising accents, in which the High stretches over two syllables, have only one of the syllables prelinked to a High. The other obtains tone by the rule of Spreading, which spreads High to the preceding mora, as shown in (44):

(44) Spreading: Spread a singly linked H to the left.

μ μ → μ μ
| \|
H   H

where μ = tone-bearing unit

Spreading is a postcyclic lexical rule which applies at Level Three. When applied to the forms in (43), its output is as in (45):[14]

Case Study: Serbo-Croatian

(45) a. Short Falling: šuma
       |
       H

b. Long Falling: zaastava
     |
     H

c. Short Rising: malina
       \\|
       H

d. Long Rising: raazlika
        \\|
        H

This rule accounts for the fact that falling accents appear only on the initial syllable — they are in fact unspread Highs. It also accounts for the fact that the final syllable cannot bear stress; due to spreading, it will never be the leftmost syllable linked to a High, which is the condition under which stress is assigned.[15]

The linked Highs that Spreading applies to are assigned lexically.[16] Not all forms are associated with tone lexically. Those that are not obtain tone by another postcyclic lexical rule, Initial High Insertion, which links a High tone to the initial mora of a toneless form (cf. Inkelas and Zec 1988):

(46) Initial High Insertion: $\begin{bmatrix} \mu & \mu_0 \end{bmatrix} \longrightarrow \begin{bmatrix} \mu & \mu_0 \\ | & \\ H & \end{bmatrix}$

Due to this rule, every form that undergoes lexical rules (which includes all and only major lexical categories) leaves the lexical component linked to tone.

In what follows I adopt this analysis, with one modification. There is no need to assume that the distribution of tone should be delegated to the underlying form and handled by means of prelinking. In fact, the distribution of tone is also predictable, although not from stress. First, in a number of forms tone is systematically 'attracted' by short syllables and 'repelled' by the long ones. Next, tone regularly appears at the right edge of a readily definable domain within stems, and this domain is properly delimited by what we independently motivate to be Level Two of the lexical component. This set of predictable properties suggests that prelinking is not an adequate device for capturing the distribution of tone, and that, instead, tone assignment should be viewed as a rule-governed process. If we adopt this view, a number of predictions follow, pertaining both to the behavior of various nominal, adjectival and verbal accentual classes, as well as to the dominant, recessive, and post-accenting behavior of certain affixes.

In order to capture what is predictable in the distribution of tone, I propose a cyclic tone linking rule which operates at Level Two and is responsible for a good part of the tonal array in Serbo-Croatian. Thus, the entire inventory of lexical tonal rules assumed here is as in (47):[17]

(47) Level One: —
      Level Two: Tone Linking Rule
      Level Three: Spreading, Initial High Insertion

This brings us back to the issue of why there are no tonal rules at Level One, and whether this violates the Strong Domain Hypothesis. As suggested earlier, the explanation is that tone assignment requires the presence of syllables, and syllables are not available until Level Two. It will be shown in the next subsection that the cyclic tone linking rule crucially makes reference to syllable structure, which makes it compatible with Level Two but not with Level One.

5.4.2 Tone Linking Rule

As we just noted, the rule to be proposed is a tone linking rule, which means that at some point tone will have to be represented as unlinked, or floating. This is precisely what will be proposed in the present subsection.

Lexical forms, both stems and affixes, can be, but do not have to be affiliated with tone in their lexical representation. This corresponds to the well-known bifurcation into accented and unaccented stems found in pitch accent languages (in the analyses of Sanskrit and Lithuanian in Kiparsky 1973 and Kiparsky and Halle 1977, as well as Poser's 1984b analysis of Japanese). Next, as already mentioned, High tone is the only tonal value to be specified in the underlying form as well as throughout the lexical levels.

Thus, lexical forms are affiliated with *floating* tone — that is,

Case Study: Serbo-Croatian   131

with a floating High tone, and we find the following types of forms in the lexical representation:

(48) a. stem   b. stem

                    |
                    H

(49) a. aff   b. aff

                   |
                   H

Tone then gets linked by rule (50), which applies at Level Two of the lexical phonology. This is only an informal statement of this rule; a more formal characterization will be given later in this subsection.

(50) Tone Linking Rule: Link the floating tone to the final syllable of the stem if and only if it does not branch.

At this point I will illustrate only briefly the effect of this rule, which is to link tone to a stem-final syllable if it is short, as in (51): tone is linked on the stem cycle to the final vowel of the stem.[18]

(51) [[maram] a] ⟶ màrama
              |
              H

If the stem-final vowel is long, as in (52), tone will fail to link at the 'stem' cycle, and will be linked to the suffix, on the next higher cycle:

(52) [[violiin]a] ⟶ violína
              |
              H

This behavior is characteristic both of simple and of derived stems, all of which can be accounted for in terms of the Tone Linking Rule.

Several important points need to be made about this rule. First, Level Two is a cyclic level, and therefore Tone Linking is a cyclic rule which starts applying on the first phonological cycle, prior to any Level Two affixation. However, although this rule applies cyclically, it does not assign more than one High to a form. This is due to the convention in (53):

(53) A floating High is deleted when it is adjacent to another High.

We will find two types of cases covered by the convention in (53). First, if both the stem and the affix are affiliated with tone, the resulting complex form will be affiliated with a single floating tone. This situation, schematized in (54):

(54) [stem] ⟶ [[stem] aff]] ⟶ [stem aff]

     H   H H   H

Second, if the affix with a floating tone is added to a stem linked to High, the floating tone is again lost. This is the kind of situation to be found at Level Two, after Tone Linking has had a chance to apply.

(55) [stem] ⟶ [[stem] aff] ⟶ [stem aff]
      | | |
     H   H H   H

A third type of case comes about when a toneless stem combines with an affix affiliated with tone. In this case, the entire derived form comes to be affiliated with tone, behaving on a par with simple stems:

(56) [stem] ⟶ [stem [aff]] ⟶ [stem aff]

                  H   H

The Tone Linking Rule is the only rule of tone assignment in the cyclic part of the lexical component. Yet, together with the postcyclic rules, it is sufficient to account for all the regularities in the distribution of Serbo-Croatian accent. In order to formulate the Tone Linking Rule more formally, and show how it functions,

Case Study: Serbo-Croatian

we will have to address the issue of what counts as the tone-bearing unit in Serbo-Croatian.

Both postcyclic rules that we discussed in the preceding subsection can be stated solely in terms of moras, and one of them, Spreading, cannot be stated in any other terms. Thus, the mora is the tone-bearing unit at the postcyclic lexical level, that is, at Level Three. But is it the tone-bearing unit at the cyclic lexical level as well?

The cyclic lexical rule of tone linking makes reference to syllable structure: tone is linked to a short but not to a long syllable. This might suggest that, at least at the cyclic level, the tone-bearing unit is the syllable – but does not resolve the problem of why only some syllables can perform this role. I will pursue a different path here, proposing that the mora is the tone-bearing unit at all phonological levels, both lexical and postlexical. The relevant difference will come from another source. I adopt the proposal made in Inkelas 1988a that only those phonological entities can bear tone that possess tonal nodes; and that, furthermore, tonal nodes are assigned not automatically, but by rule. In other words, by claiming that mora is the tone bearing unit, we are in fact claiming that tonal nodes are assigned only to moras, although not necessarily to all moras.

We noted earlier that the Tone Linking Rule links tone to short syllables but not to long ones. In order to account for this fact and at the same time retain the mora as the tone bearing unit, I propose that only those moras that act as syllable heads are assigned tonal nodes.

The representation of syllable-internal structure we have been utilizing here is as in (57):

(57)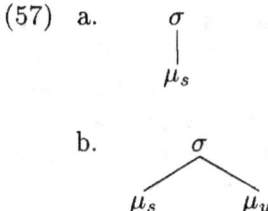

Rule (58) assigns tonal nodes to those moras that act as heads of the syllable, that is, those that carry the s label, yielding (59) and (60):

(58) Tonal Node Assignment (Level Two):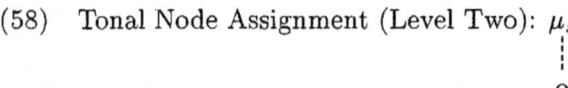

(59)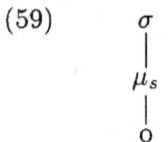

(60)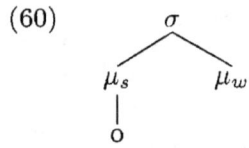

In view of this, we can restate the Tone Linking Rule as in (61), and then formulate it as in (62):

(61) Tone Linking Rule [final version]: Link the floating tone to the rightmost mora of the stem if it is linked to a tonal node.

(62) Tone Linking Rule: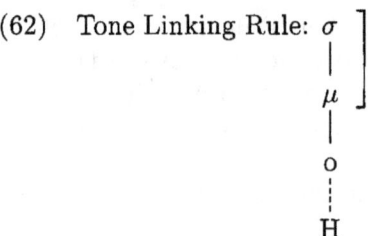

Note that only the single head of a short syllable will ever appear in this position; a long final syllable will fail to meet the structural description of the Tone Linking Rule, which explains why this rule never links tone to the head of a long syllable.

We saw that only the Tone Linking Rule is affected by the restriction as to which moras can act as tone-bearing units. Spreading can operate on any mora, whether it is the syllable head or not. This suggests that at some point *all* moras obtain tonal nodes. Thus, in addition to the rule of Tonal Node Assignment that applies at Level Two, we also find a postcyclic default rule which operates across the board, assigning tonal nodes to all moras that

Case Study: Serbo-Croatian

have not already obtained a tonal node by the earlier rule. This rule is not sensitive to syllable structure, and assigns a tonal node to any mora, regardless of the label it carries.

(63) Default Tonal Node Assignment (Level Three): μ
$$\vdots$$
$$o$$

This default rule applies postcyclically, that is at Level Three. It will certainly have to apply before Spreading, which is completely oblivious to syllable structure and can affect any mora. The rule of Initial High Insertion assigns tone to the first mora in the phonological word. Since this mora is also syllable initial, and therefore head of the syllable, it is assigned a tonal node by the cyclic rule. Thus, Initial High Insertion does not crucially interact with Default Tonal Node Assignment.

In principle, it would be desirable for this, or any other, default rule to apply at its level as early as possible; and all the facts that we know of are consistent with the assumption that Default Tonal Node Assignment applies before all other Level Three rules.

5.5 Underived Forms

5.5.1 Nominal Stems

Traditionally, nominal stems are classified into barytone, that is, those that have accent on the stem; oxytone, whose accent is on the ending; and mobile stems, whose declensions contain forms of both kinds (see Illich-Svitych 1979). In our terms, the mobile class consists of toneless stems, while stems of both the barytone and the oxytone classes are lexically affiliated with tone.

Recall that Tone Linking Rule is sensitive to the vowel length in the stem final syllable. In a sense, this rule yields a classification of stems into those that end in a syllable with a long vowel, and those that end in a syllable with a short vowel. This classification is orthogonal to the classification into barytone, oxytone, and mobile stems. It is interesting to note that, if we conflate these two classifications, it becomes obvious that there is a gap in the paradigm. In particular, while the class with a short stem-final syllable includes barytone, oxytone, and mobile stems, the class with a long stem-final syllable includes oxytone and mobile, but no barytone stems. This is schematized in (64):

(64)

	barytone	oxytone	mobile
'short'	yes	yes	yes
'long'	no	yes	yes

The gap in the 'long' class is not an accident. We will now show that it follows from the operation of the Tone Linking Rule.

We will first look at the barytone and oxytone nouns of the productive type. The relevant paradigms for the barytone class are given in (65)-(67).[19] Note that all the forms in this class have a short vowel in the stem-final syllable.[20]

(65) Masculine Barytone

	Singular	Plural
Nom	jèlen	jèlen-i
Acc	jèlen-a	jèlen-e
Gen	jèlen-a	jḗlēn-a
Dat	jèlen-u	jèlen-ima
Ins	jèlen-om	jèlen-ima
Loc	jèlen-u	jèlen-ima

(66) Feminine Barytone

	Singular	Plural
Nom	bùndev-a	bùndev-e
Acc	bùndev-u	bùndev-e
Gen	bùndev-e	bűndēv-a
Dat	bùndev-i	bùndev-ama
Ins	bùndev-om	bùndev-ama
Loc	bùndev-i	bùndev-ama

(67) Neuter Barytone

	Singular	Plural
Nom	kòlen-o	kòlen-a
Acc	kòlen-o	kòlen-a
Gen	kòlen-a	kőlēn-a
Dat	kòlen-u	kòlen-ima
Ins	kòlen-om	kòlen-ima
Loc	kòlen-u	kòlen-ima

Case Study: Serbo-Croatian

In (68)-(70) are listed the relevant oxytone forms. Here, the stem-final syllable regularly contains a long vowel, in contrast to what we saw in the barytone class.[21]

(68) Masculine Oxytone

	Singular	Plural
Nom	jùnāk	junác-i
Acc	junák-a	junák-e
Gen	junák-a	junák-a
Dat	junák-u	junác-ima
Ins	junák-om	junác-ima
Loc	junák-u	junác-ima

(69) Feminine Oxytone

	Singular	Plural
Nom	violín-a	violín-e
Acc	violín-u	violín-e
Gen	violín-e	violín-a
Dat	violín-i	violín-ama
Ins	violín-om	violín-ama
Loc	violín-i	violín-ama

(70) Neuter Oxytone

	Singular	Plural
Nom	načél-o	načél-a
Acc	načél-o	načél-a
Gen	načél-a	načél-a
Dat	načél-u	načél-ima
Ins	načél-om	načél-ima
Loc	načél-u	načél-ima

The Tone Linking Rule alone derives all these forms. In order to demonstrate this, let us take one form of the barytone class, and one of the oxytone class. As we said earlier, both these forms are affiliated with tone.

(71) maram 'scarf'   (Barytone)

   H

(72) violiin 'violin'   (Oxytone)

   H

The derivations proceed as follows. Since Tone Linking starts prior to any Level Two affixation, in the case of simple stems it operates on the stem-final syllable. This explains the difference in accentual pattern between the two types of stems, as shown in (73):[22]

(73)

		Barytone	Oxytone
Input to Level 2:		[maram]	[violiin]
		H	H

Cycle 1	Tone Linking:	[maram]
		    |
		    H
			–

Cycle 2	Morphology:	[maram] a
		   |
		   H
			[violiin] a
			
			H

Cycle 2	Tone Linking:	–	[violiin] a
			      |
			      H

Input to Level 3:		[marama]
		  |
		  H
			[violiina]
			   |
			   H

	Spreading:	[marama]
		  ↘
		  H
			[violiina]
			   ↘
			   H

Only the stem in the left column, *maram-* 'scarf', can undergo Tone Linking on Cycle One; the stem in the righthand column, *violiin-* 'violin', which ends in a long vowel, does not meet the structural description of the rule on this cycle. However, this latter stem can undergo Tone Linking at Cycle Two, where it obtains the inflectional ending.[23] After Spreading has applied at Level Three, we get the High tone contours identical to those in the surface form.

In sum, Tone Linking dinstinguishes between the 'short' stems that ca be linked to tone, and the 'long' stems, which exhibit a 'post-accenting' behavior. This places all 'long' stems in the oxytone class, and 'short' stems in the barytone class.[24]

Below are listed examples of polysyllabic barytone and oxytone stems of all three genders. Both these classes are highly productive.

(74) Polysyllabic barytone stems:

masculine
čòvek/čòvek-a 'man'
jèlen/jèlen-a 'deer'
cìrkus/cìrkus-a 'circus'
ìzvor/ìzvor-a 'source'
šàran/šàran-a 'carp'
tènis/tènis-a 'tennis'
karànfil/karànfil-a 'carnation'
kukùruz/kukùruz-a 'corn'
bùbreg/bùbreg-a 'kidney'
prózor/prózor-a 'window'
čèlik/čèlik-a 'steel'
bìser/bìser-a 'pearl'
šèćer/šèćer-a 'sugar'
vàlcer/vàlcer-a 'waltz'

feminine
lìvad-a 'meadow'
màlin-a 'rasberry'
tàrab-a 'fence'
kòlib-a 'cottage'
pàprik-a 'pepper'
pìjac-a 'market'
čàrap-a 'stocking'
harmònik-a 'accordion'
pšènic-a 'wheat'
bùndev-a 'pumpkin'
ćèlij-a 'cell'
fàbrik-a 'factory'
mùzik-a 'music'
prírod-a 'nature'

neuter
òlov-o 'lead'
kòrit-o 'barrel'
gòved-o 'cattle'
kòlen-o 'knee'
kòpit-o 'hoof'
pròleć-e 'spring'

(75) Polysyllabic stems of the oxytone class

    masculine   *feminine*
    jùnak/junák-a 'hero'   Argentı́n-a 'Argentina'
    krìstal/kristál-a 'crystal'   gitár-a 'guitar'
    hàjduk/hajdúk-a 'outlaw'   galám-a 'noise'
    ofìcir/oficír-a 'officer'   sezón-a 'season'
    mètal/metál-a 'metal'   apoték-a 'pharmacy'

    neuter
    načél-o 'principle'
    odél-o 'clothing'

Moreover, given the formulation of the Tone Linking Rule, we would expect that monosyllables affiliated with tone will fall into two classes as well: those with a short syllable should belong to the barytone class, and those with a long syllable to the oxytone class. This is exactly what we find, as illustrated by the example in (76) and (77).

(76) Monosyllabic barytone stems

    masculine   *feminine*   *neuter*
    bĕg/bĕg-a 'beg'   knjĭg-a 'book'   jŭtr-o 'morning'
    jăd/jăd-a 'woe'   šŭm-a 'forest'   čŭd-o 'miracle'
    skŭp/skŭp-a 'set'   kŭć-a 'house'   gr̆l-o 'throat'
    pr̆st/pr̆st-a 'finger'   krăv-a 'cow'   lĕt-o 'summer'

(77) Monosyllabic stems of the oxytone class

    masculine   *feminine*   *neuter*
    krâlj/králj-a 'king'   cén-a 'price'   pı́sm-o 'letter'
    kljûč/kljúč-a 'key'   lúk-a 'harbor'   br̄vn-o 'log'
    dvôr/dvór-a 'court'   rék-a 'river'   crév-o 'intestine'
    nôž/nóž-a 'knife'   tém-a 'topic'   jézgr-o 'core'
    lêk/lék-a 'medicine'   zvézd-a 'star'   súkn-o 'cloth'

In addition to the productive oxytone class of stems whose final syllable contains a long vowel, there is also a class of oxytone stems with a short vowel in the final syllable. The relevant paradigms are given in (78)-(80):

Case Study: Serbo-Croatian

(78) Masculine Oxytone ('short')

	Singular	Plural
Nom	svèdok	svedòc-i
Acc	svedòk-a	svedòk-e
Gen	svedòk-a	svedók-a
Dat	svedòk-u	svedòc-ima
Ins	svedòk-om	svedòc-ima
Loc	svedòk-u	svedòc-ima

(79) Feminine Oxytone ('short')

	Singular	Plural
Nom	teràs-a	teràs-e
Acc	teràs-u	teràs-e
Gen	teràs-e	terás-a
Dat	teràs-i	teràs-ama
Ins	teràs-om	teràs-ama
Loc	teràs-i	teràs-ama

(80) Neuter Oxytone ('short')

	Singular	Plural
Nom	vretèn-o	vretèn-a
Acc	vretèn-o	vretèn-a
Gen	vretèn-a	vretén-a
Dat	vretèn-u	vretèn-ima
Ins	vretèn-om	vretèn-ima
Loc	vretèn-u	vretèn-ima

Thus, nouns like *svedok* 'witness', *terasa* 'balcony', or *vreteno* 'spindle' all have a short vowel in stem-final syllable but still fail to get tone linked to the final syllable of the stem. This class of oxytone nouns is very small, in contrast to the other, highly productive class. I will assume that TLR fails to apply in this case because of the interfering effect of a blocking process.

The blocking effect will be attributed to the tonal tier. In particular, nouns of this class will be treated here as affiliated with a floating tone marked for extraprosodicity (for a proposal to represent tone as extrametrical, see Inkelas (forthcoming)).

(81) svedok

(H)

Being extraprosodic, the floating tone will be invisible to TLR, and the rule will fail to apply on the 'stem' cycle. On the next higher cycle, where inflectional endings are added, extraprosodicity is lost: the complex stem will now undergo Tone Linking, which links tone to the inflectional ending. The derivation of a nouns like *svedok* is given in (82):

(82) *Input to Level 2:*   [svedok]

            (H)

   Cycle 1 Tone Linking: –

   Cycle 2 Morphology: [svedok] a]

                                              H
   Cycle 2 Tone Linking: [svedok]a
                                       |
                                       H

   Output: svedoka
                                  |
                                  H

Below are listed the polysyllabic nouns that belong to this class. As already mentioned, this class is very small; the listing given below is practically exhaustive.

(83) Polysyllabic
   masculine   *feminine*
   svèdok/svedòk-a 'witness'   aždàja 'dragon'
   žìvot/živòt-a 'life'   adrèsa 'address'
   jàglac/jaglàc-a 'narcissus'   ankèta 'questionnare'
   màdrac/madràc-a 'mattress' kravàta 'tie'
                                               romànsa 'romance'
   neuter   teràsa 'terrace'
   vretèn-o   paralèla 'parallel'

Furthermore, we again find a class of monosyllabic forms that behave in exactly the same way.

(84) Monosyllabic

masculine	feminine	neuter
kŏnj/kònj-a 'horse'	žèn-a 'woman'	tàn-e 'bullet'
rŏb/ròb-a 'slave'	bòj-a 'color'	srèbr-o 'silver'
gȑč/gȑč-a 'spasm'	lùl-a 'pipe'	staklo 'glass'
tŏp/tòp-a 'canon'	kàf-a 'coffee'	vèdr-o 'tub'
mȁč/màč-a 'sword'	pàra 'coin',	pèr-o 'feather'
snŏp/snòp-a 'bushel'	čèsma 'fountain'	rèbr-o 'rib'
lȅš/lèš-a 'corpse'		

Having examined the barytone and the oxytone stems, we now turn to the mobile stems. In our terms, these forms are unaffiliated with tone, and as such do not undergo Tone Linking. However, another factor comes into play; although toneless, these stems can obtain tone from the ending, as shown by the following paradigm:

(85) Masculine Mobile

	Singular	Plural
Nom	zûb	zûb-i
Acc	zûb	zûb-e
Gen	zûb-a	zúb-a
Dat	zûb-u	zúb-ima
Ins	zûb-om	zúb-ima
Loc	zúb-u	zúb-ima

The paradigm in (85) contains forms with a falling and with a rising accent. Those with a falling accent combine with a toneless ending; they remain toneless throughout the cyclic domain and eventually receive tone by virtue of the Initial High Insertion. Forms with a rising accent combine with an accented ending and receive tone by Tone Linking.

The pattern of masculine endings, and their affiliation with tone is given in (86):[25]

(86) Masculine endings:

	Singular	Plural
Nom	ă	i
Acc	ă/a	e
Gen	a	i H
Dat	u	ima H
Ins	om	ima H
Loc	u/u H	ima H

Let us now look at the derivation of a form which combines with a toneless ending, and of a form whose ending is affiliated with tone.

(87) *Input to Level 2:*   [zuub]   [zuub]

    Cycle 1   Tone Linking: —   —

    Cycle 2   Morphology: [zuub] i   [zuub] ima

                                                                H

    Cycle 2   Tone Linking: –   [zuub] ima
                                                                 H

    Input to Level 3:   [zuub] i   [zuubima]
                                                                    H

            Initial High: [zuub] i   [zuubima]
                                       H   H

Thus, toneless underived forms will surface with cyclically assigned tone only if the inflectional ending they combine with has its own tone. If a stem leaves the cyclic component unattached to tone, it will obtain tone by Initial High Insertion, a postcyclic rule which operates on toneless stems. Thus, no content word will

Case Study: Serbo-Croatian

leave the lexicon unlinked to tone; under certain assumptions in lexical phonology (Kiparsky 1982a,b, also Inkelas and Zec 1988) only content words undergo lexical rules.

In sum, a single cyclic tonal rule accounts for three classes of stems: the mobile class, which consists of toneless forms; the barytone class, which undergoes Tone Linking at the 'stem' cycle; and the oxytone class which does not meet the structural description of Tone Linking, and therefore exhibits a 'post-accenting' behavior.

5.6 Derived Forms

Recall that Tone Linking sets apart two large classes of stems — those that end in a short syllable and have tone linked to the stem, and those that end in a long syllable and exhibit 'post-accenting' behavior.

This generalization is not limited to simple stems. It extends to the derived stems, which also exhibit 'post-accenting' behavior if their final syllable is long.

In this section we look at nominal and adjectival derived forms. The behavior of simple stems with respect to the tone linking rule suggests two relevant dimensions in determining the accentual behavior of suffixes — one being whether the suffix is affiliated with tone, and the other whether it contains a long or a short vowel. These two properties yield four types of suffixes:

(88) a. accented, short final syllable
 b. accented, long final syllable
 c. unaccented, short final syllable
 d. unaccented, long final syllable

We can further specify at which of the two cyclic levels the suffix is added, which yields a third, orthogonal, dimension — and a final count of eight suffix classes.

5.6.1 Accented Suffixes

I will first focus on accented suffixes, which appear both at Level One and at Level Two. At Level One they behave like dominant suffixes, and at Level Two they behave like recessive suffixes. Furthermore, those with a long syllable have a post-accenting behavior, just like the simple stems of the same form. But there will be no need to make reference to the dominant, recessive, or post-accenting properties of any of these suffixes. Their behavior will follow from the Tone Linking rule already motivated for simple stems.

The suffixes listed in (89) will be used to illustrate this set of properties:

(89) a. Level One, accented, short:
-*at* [dominant]
b. Level One, accented, long:
-*aaš* [dominant, post-accenting]
c. Level Two, accented, short:
-*ic* [recessive]
d. Level Two, accented, long:
-*aar* [recessive, post-accenting]

We will start with Level One suffixes. Recall that the Tone Linking Rule operates before any Level Two morphological processes have taken place; and crucially, after all Level One processes have applied. Therefore, crucial for the operation of the Tone Linking Rule are the properties of the *final* Level One suffix added to the stem before it proceeds to Level Two.

If the stem ends in a suffix with a short syllable, for example the suffix -*at* which combines with nominal stems to form adjectives (listed in (89)a), the rule will link tone to the suffix. This happens regardless of what type of stem the suffix is added to.

When -*at* is added to a toneless stem, the tone of the suffix gets to be affiliated with the entire derived form.

(90) a. nos- 'nose'
b. [[nos] at]
    |
    H

At Level Two, the Tone Linking Rule links High to the final syllable, i.e. to the syllable belonging to the suffix, since it is short:

(91) [nosat] ⟶ [nosat] (nòsat)
      | |
      H   H

If -*at* is added to an accented stem, as in (92)a, due to con-

Case Study: Serbo-Croatian

vention (67), the entire domain will have only one High whatever the number of Highs introduced lexically, yielding (92)b.

(92) a. [[braad]+ at]

          H   H
   b. [[braad]+ at]

               H

The form in (92b) then enters Level Two and undergoes Tone Linking:[26]

(93) [braadat] (bràdat)
          |
         H

Thus, tone will always be linked to the suffix, regardless of what type of stem it is added to. Crucially, if more than one suffix of this class is added to the stem, given the functioning of the Tone Linking Rule, we predict that tone will be linked to the rightmost one. This is precisely what happens, as shown in (94), where the comparative-forming suffix -*ij* comes after - *at*:[27]

(94) [braadatij-] (bradàtiji)
           |
         H

We will now turn to Level One suffixes with a long syllable. When a suffix of this class appears stem-finally at the point when Tone Linking applies, the application of this rule is blocked. However, since the suffix is accented, the derived stem will eventually receive tone at the first higher cycle that meets the structural description of Tone Linking. Again, this will happen regardless of the accentual behavior of the stem that the suffix is added to: if this stem is toneless, it will receive tone from the suffix, and if it is accented its tone will merge with that of the suffix by virtue of the principle in (16).

The suffix -*aaš*, listed in (90)b as a dominant post-accenting suffix, can be added either to an unaccented stem, as in (95), or to an accented stem, as in (96):

(95) a. kaart- 'card'
 b. [[kaart] aaš]

          H

(96) a. harmon i k- 'accordion'

            H
 b. [[harmonik] aaš]

        H   H

In both cases, tone is linked at a cycle higher than that at which -*aaš* is added, as shown in (97) by the derivation of forms containing the two types of accented Level One suffixes:

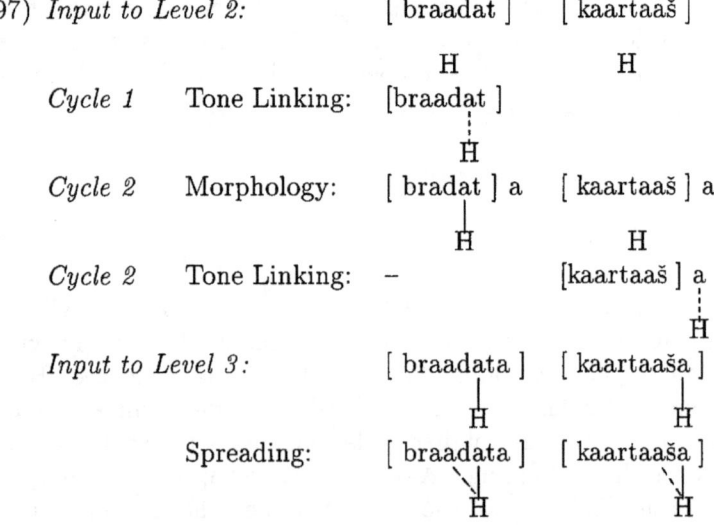

In sum, accented Level One suffixes are dominant if they contain a short syllable, and post-accenting dominant if they contain a long syllable.

Case Study: Serbo-Croatian

Level Two suffixes are always added after at least one application of Tone Linking, which explains their recessive behavior.

The suffix -*ic*, listed in (89)c as an accented recessive suffix, is added to feminine nouns to form diminutives. Let us first see what happens when this suffix is added to nouns ending in a short syllable. With unaccented stems tone is linked to the suffix, as in (98)a, and with accented stems it is linked to the stem, as in (99)b.

(98) a. vodica 'water-Dim' (vòdica)
       |
       H

 b. maramica 'scarf-Dim' (màramica)
       |
       H

The derivations of these two stems are given in (99):

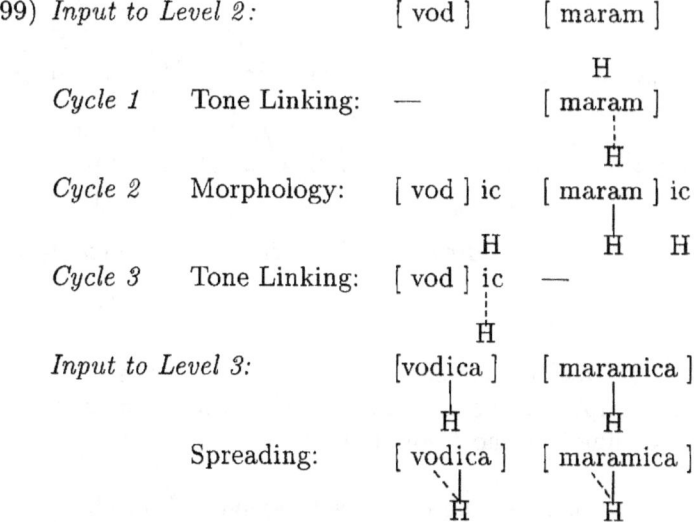

With stems ending in a long vowel, the situation is somewhat different. Even though Tone Linking does operate before the suffix -*ic* is added, it fails to link tone to the stem's final vowel, which is long. This neutralizes the distinction between the accented and unaccented stems with a final long vowel, as shown in (100); see the derivations in (101):

(100) a. glaav- 'head' ⟶ glaavica (glàvica)
              |
              H

b. traav- 'grass' ⟶ traavica (tràvica)
   | |
   H   H

Below are given the derivations of these forms:

(101) *Input to Level 2:*   [glaav]   [traav]
                                                    |
                                                    H

Cycle 1   Tone Linking: —   —

Cycle 2   Morphology: [glaav] ic   [traav] ic
                                          H   H
Cycle 2   Tone Linking: [glaav] ic   [traav] ic
                                          ⋮   ⋮
                                          H   H

Cycle 3   Morphology: [glaavic] a [traavic] a
                                          ⋮   ⋮
                                          H   H

Input to Level 3:   [glavica]   [travica]
                                        | |
                                        H   H

            Spreading: [glavica]   [travica]
                                        ↘   ↘
                                        H   H

The fourth and final type of accented suffix is post-accenting recessive, exemplified here by *-aar*, which forms agentive nouns. For stems ending in a short vowel, we have:

(102) a. brod- 'ship' ⟶ brodaara 'sailor-Gen/Sg' (brodára)
                                |
                                H

b. rib- 'fish' ⟶ ribaara 'fisherman-Gen/Sg'
   | |
   H   H

Case Study: Serbo-Croatian

Again, a suffix with a long vowel acts as post-accenting, although not in all cases: when added to nouns of the barytone class, this suffix exhibits recessive behavior. The derivations of these forms are given in (103):

(103) Input to Level 2:   [brod]   [rib]

                                                          H

      Cycle 1   Tone Linking: —   [rib]
                                                     H

      Cycle 2   Morphology: [brod] aar [rib] aar
                                                           H   H H

      Cycle 2   Tone Linking: —   —

      Cycle 3   Morphology: [brodaar]a [ribaar]a
                                                         H   H

      Cycle 3   Tone Linking: [brodaar]a   —
                                                              H

      Input to Level 3:   [brodaara] [ribaara]
                                                              H   H

                 Spreading: [brodaara] [ribaara]
                                                              H   H

And, a final pattern to look at is what happens with long stems. We again find a neutralization between those stems that are toneless and those that have their own tone, as shown in the derivation in (104):

(104) Input to Level 2:   [zuub]   [viin]
                                                       |
                                                       H

    Cycle 1   Tone Linking: —   —

    Cycle 2   Morphology: [zuub] aar   [viin] aar
                                                       |
                                      H   H

    Cycle 2   Tone Linking: —   —

    Cycle 3   Morphology: [zuubaar] a   [viinaar] a
                                      H   H
    Cycle 3   Tone Linking: [zuubaar] a   [viinaar] a
                                             | |
                                             H   H

    Input to Level 3:   [zubaara]   [vinaara]
                                          | |
                                          H   H

    Spreading: [zubaara]   [vinaara]
                                        ↘   ↘
                                          H   H

5.6.2 Unaccented Suffixes

Just like the accented suffixes, the unaccented ones are also found both at Level One and at Level Two. The cases we go through in this subsection are listed in (105). I have not found any examples of one of the predicted cases, unaccented Level One suffixes with a long vowel. All Level One suffixes with a long vowel that I have been able to find appear to be accented, and I will assume that this represents an accidental gap in the paradigm.

(105) a. Level One, unaccented, short:
         -en [dependent]
      b. Level One, unaccented, long:
         —
      c. Level Two, unaccented, short:
         -ov/-ev [recessive]
      d. Level Two, unaccented, long:
         -aad [recessive, dependent]

Level One suffixes which contain a short vowel (type (105)a) create two accentual classes. When added to toneless stems they

Case Study: Serbo-Croatian

form a derived toneless stem which fails to undergo Tone Linking; when added to a stem with tone they form a derived stem whose tone is linked at Level Two to the suffix. An example is the adjective-forming suffix *-en*, which is added to nominal stems. The table in (106) lists the two types of derived stems formed by this suffix:[28]

(106) Accented   Unaccented
       lan-èn   vȍd-en
       vun-èn   lȅd-en
       pakl-èn   mȅd-en
       sukn-èn
       platn-èn
       stakl-èn
       svil-èn

When the short unaccented suffix *-en* is added to a toneless nominal stem, the resulting form is again a toneless stem, since neither of the component parts can contribute tone. This form will leave the cyclic component unlinked to tone, and will therefore be assigned tone by Initial High Insertion. Thus, it will surface with tone linked to the initial syllable:

(107) [[vod] en]

But when a short unaccented suffix is added to a stem affiliated with tone, as in (108), the entire derived stem will be affiliated with the tone of the nominal form, and will undergo Tone Linking:

(108) [[lan] en] ⟶ [lanen]
                              |
       H   H

The derivations of these forms are given in (109):

(109) *Level One*   Morphology: [lan] en   [led] en

                                       H
       Level Two   Tone Linking: [lanen]   —
                                       |
                                       H

       Level Three Initial High: —   [leden]
                                                    |
                                                    H

If there were long unaccented suffixes at Level One, they would be expected to behave in the following way: With accented stems they would behave like post-accenting suffixes, and with unaccented stems they would have no effect on the place of accent.

We now turn to suffixes at Level Two, starting with the short suffix *ov/ev*, which is added to nouns to form possessive adjectives. When this suffix combines with a barytone stem, tone will always be linked to the stem, as in (110); this is because Tone Linking will apply before any Level Two suffixation takes place.

(110) a. brat-ov → brătov
          |
          H

      b. jelen-ov → jèlenov
           |
           H

When a short unaccented Level Two suffix is added to an oxytone stem, which, as we saw in the previous section, cannot be linked to tone at the 'stem' cycle, tone links to the suffix:

(111) a. kraalj-ev → králjev
               |
               H

      b. generaal-ov → generálov
                 |
                 H

The contrast between the forms in (110) and (111) is shown in the following derivation:

Case Study: Serbo-Croatian

(112)   *Input to Level 2*   [brat]   [kraalj]

                                      H   H
                 Tone Linking: [brat]   —
                                    H̓

       Level 2   Morphology: [brat] ov   [kraalj] ev
                                    H   H

       Level 2   Tone Linking: —   [kraalj] ev
                                                                              H̓

       Level 3   Initial High: —   —

Finally, if the suffix is added to a toneless stem, Tone Linking Tone Linking does not apply, and the entire form undergoes Initial High Insertion, surfacing with tone on the initial syllable. The derivation of the form in (113) is given in (114).

(113) dever-ov → děverov

(114)   *Input to Level 2*   [dever]

                    Tone Linking: —

      Level 2   Morphology: [dever] ov

      Level 2   Tone Linking: —

      Level 3   Initial High: [deverov]
                                                      H̓

Finally, for Level Two unaccented suffixes with a long vowel we predict that they should yield three accentual classes. We take as an example the suffix *-aad*. When this suffix combines with a barytone stem, tone will be linked to the stem, as shown in (115), where this suffix is added to the stem *unuk-* 'grandchild'.

(115) unučaad   ùnučaad
       |
       H

When the stem is toneless, Tone Linking fails to apply, and the entire stem undergoes Initial High Insertion at Level Three. An example of this type of case is given in (116), with the toneless form *pastorǎk* 'stepchild':

(116) pastorčaad   pastorčaad
      |
     H

The third type of case predicted by our analysis is that of an oxytone stem combined with this suffix. The expected pattern is that tone will fail to link either to the stem or to the suffix; that is, that it is only at the point that the inflectional ending is added that tone will eventually be linked, and that the target of linking will be the inflectional ending itself. However, I have not found any cases of *-aad* combined with an oxytone stem. This seems to be a gap in the paradigm.[29]

The derivations with the barytone and toneless stems are given in (117):

(117) Input to Level 2   [unuk]   [pastorǎk]

                              H

        Tone Linking: [unuk]   —
                            Ḣ

        Morphology: [unuk] aad [pastorǎk] aad
                            Ḣ

        Tone Linking: —   —

Level 3 Initial High: —   [pastorčaad]
                                    Ḣ

5.7 Adjectival Stems

The Tone Linking Rule accounts for the adjectival accentual patterns as naturally as it does for the nominal ones. Without any additions to the present inventory of formal devices, we will be able to characterize the definiteness distinction among adjectives, which is manifested as a difference in accent.

The most significant fact to note is that adjectives form two inflectional classes, the definite and the indefinite. We will not attempt here to delimit the class of stems that exhibit this alternation. It seems in fact that the semantic properties of the stem are crucial in determining its compatibility with the definiteness distinction, and this area is outside the scope of the present discussion. In this section I mostly focus on stems that do exhibit the definiteness distinction, and only mention only in passing some of those that do not.

In order to illustrate the definiteness distinction, we will take the adjective *zelen* 'green' and see how it declines in its masculine form; although we will limit our discussion to this set of forms, everything we say about them extends fully to the feminine and neuter forms as well. The definite and indefinite masculine declensions are given in (118) and (119) respectively:

(118) Definite (Masculine)

	Singular	*Plural*
Nom	zèlen-i	zèlen-i
Acc	zèlen-og	zèlen-e
Gen	zèlen-og	zèlen-ih
Dat	zèlen-om	zèlen-im
Ins	zèlen-im	zèlen-im
Loc	zèlen-om	zèlen-im

(119) Indefinite (Masculine)

	Singular	*Plural*
Nom	zèlen	zelèn-i
Acc	zelèn-og	zelèn-e
Gen	zelèn-og	zelèn-ih
Dat	zelèn-om	zelèn-im
Ins	zelèn-im	zelèn-im
Loc	zelèn-om	zelèn-im

Accent provides the principal difference between the two paradigms, although certain endings differ segmentally as well. The indefinite class has its accent assigned to the ending, while the definite class has the accent assigned to the stem. This becomes obvious when the forms in question are represented in our terms;

for example, the genitive singular forms of the two declensions are as in (120):[30]

(120) a. Genitive Singular Indefinite: zelen-og
            |
            H
   b. Genitive Singular Definite: zelen-og
            |
            H

In order to treat definite and indefinite adjectives as minimally distinct, that is, to preserve the intuition that they are different inflectional paradigms, I will assume that they differ only in their inflectional endings. My proposal is that the indefinite endings are affiliated with tone, and that their form is as follows:

(121) Indefinite (masculine) endings:

	Singular	Plural
Nom	ă	i
	H	H
Acc	ă/og	e
	H	H
Gen	og	ih
	H	H
Dat	om	im
	H	H
Ins	im	im
	H	H
Loc	om	im
	H	H

These endings are found both on simple and on derived adjectival stems. Although it is not easy to delimit the class of stems that exhibit the definiteness distinction, this property does correlated to some extent with the morphological properties of the stem. As

Case Study: Serbo-Croatian

noted earlier, Serbo-Croatian has two cyclic levels, and only those adjectival stems that appear at Level One can be declined for definiteness. This strongly suggests that the inflectional endings that mark definiteness are located at Level One.

This will now be shown for derived adjectival stems declinable for definiteness. These stems are of two kinds. First, we find those that are derived from roots without any category specification, by means of suffixes like -*ok* or -*ăk*.[31]

(122) a. [[vis] ok]
      b. [[niz] ăk]

Since the roots *vis* and *niz* are unspecified for category, they can obtain this specification only through the derivational processes that they undergo. The suffixes that such roots combine with all belong to Level One.

The second class of derived stems that exhibit the definiteness alternation are adjectives derived from nominal stems. Among the suffixes responsible for this are *ăn* and -*en*; the examples are given in (123) and (124).

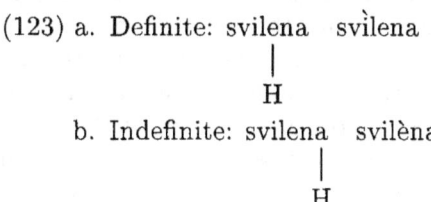

(123) a. Definite: svilena   svìlena
                              |
                              H
      b. Indefinite: svilena   svilèna
                              |
                              H

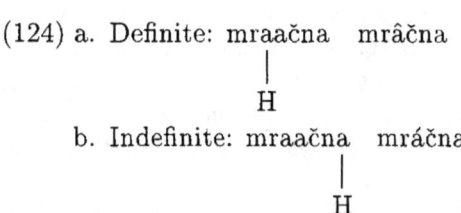

(124) a. Definite: mraačna   mrâčna
                              |
                              H
      b. Indefinite: mraačna   mráčna
                              |
                              H

Crucially, these suffixes appear at Level One. We saw in subsection 5.2.2. that the suffix -*ăn* triggers presonorant lengthening, which applies only at Level One; and we also saw that -*en* has all the properties of a Level One unaccented suffix (subsection 5.6.2). Furthermore, forms derived by adjective-forming suffixes that reside at Level Two do not exhibit the definiteness distinction, for example -*ast* and -*ăsk*.

That -*ast* is a Level Two suffix follows from the fact that it comes after another Level Two suffix, namely -*ic* (see section 5.6.1), as shown in (125):

(125) a. [[[rup] ic] ast]

        H
   b. rŭpičast 'full of holes'

The suffix -*ăsk*, one of the yer suffixes, fails to trigger trigger presonorant lengthening, as shown in section 5.2.2, which places it at Level Two; and its behavior with respect to Tone Assignment further supports this claim, as will be show in section 5.8.

An interesting correlation is found in the formation of comparative forms. The comparative-forming suffix -*ij* also appears to be at Level One; in particular, it combines with adjectives derived at Level One but not with those derived at Level Two. Thus, adjectives derived by the suffixes -*ast* and -*ăsk* fail to combine with the comparative ending; for example, although color terms are generally capable of having comparative forms, the adjective *narandžast* 'orange' does not have a comparative form, as shown by the ill-formed *narandžastiji. Moreover, the suffix -*ij* is affiliated with tone, and its behavior with respect to Tone Linking further supports our hypothesis that it is a Level One suffix. It behaves like a dominant suffix, just like the other accented Level One suffixes with a short vowel (see section 5.6.1).

Following this analogy, I will assume that the indefinite adjectival endings also appear at Level One. Several things are gained by this assumption. First, we delimit the class of derived adjectival forms that obtain the definiteness marking. Second, we account for the fact that the indefinite endings always get tone, whether they combine with a toneless stem or not.

In (126) are given derivations of three indefinite adjectival forms, one simplex and two complex.

Case Study: Serbo-Croatian

(126) Level 1   zelen   sviil   mraak

                                H
Morphology   —   [sviil] en   [mraak] ăn

Other rules   —   —   [mraač] n

Morphology   [zelen] og [sviilen] og [mraačn] og

                              H   H   H
Level 2

Tone Linking [zelen og] [sviilen og] [mraačn og]
                     ⋮   ⋮   ⋮
                     H   H   H

Thus indefinite endings exhibit dominant behavior, just like the comparative suffix, which we have shown to be at Level One.

We now turn to the definite paradigm. To foreshadow the analysis to be proposed, the inflectional endings that we find on the definite forms are assigned at Level Two. These endings will not be treated as specifically associated with the definite forms. Rather, the proposal is that they will be added to any adjectival form that has not been inflected from some other source. In sum, the general adjectival inflection is located at Level Two, while the indefinite inflection, which is more specific, appears at Level One. This is reminiscent of the distinction between, say, the strong and weak preterite inflections in English, which have a comparable distribution across levels; the less productive inflectional form is associated with a lower level (Kiparsky 1982a,b).

The definite paradigm poses a further problem. Unlike the indefinite forms, the definite ones have tone linked to the stem. Furthermore, this is true both of stems with their own tone, and of those that are toneless. It appears in fact that the source of the [+definite] marking is the accent itself: to capture this, I propose that the [+ definite] feature is contributed by a tonal derivational suffix, which creates definite adjectival forms:

(127) [+ def]

      H

This suffix will also be at Level One. The reason for assuming this is that its tone is linked at the 'stem' cycle, that is, before any inflectional endings are added. This will be possible only if the suffix is added before the first application of Tone Linking, which operates at Level Two.

In (128) are listed the adjectival endings of the Level Two paradigm, that is, the class of default endings. As shown in (128), these endings are toneless, as distinct from the indefinite class.

(128) Default masculine endings (first approximation):

	Singular	Plural
Nom	i	i
Acc	i/og	e
Gen	og	ih
Dat	om	im
Ins	im	im
Loc	om	im

In (129) and (130) are given derivations of an in definite and a definite form respectively. The accentual difference is expressed as a difference in levels; indefinite endings, which behave like 'dominant' suffixes, appear at Level One, while the default set of endings, which exhibit a 'recessive' behavior, appear at Level Two.

(129) *Level 1*   [zelen]

              Morphology: [zelen] og [–def]

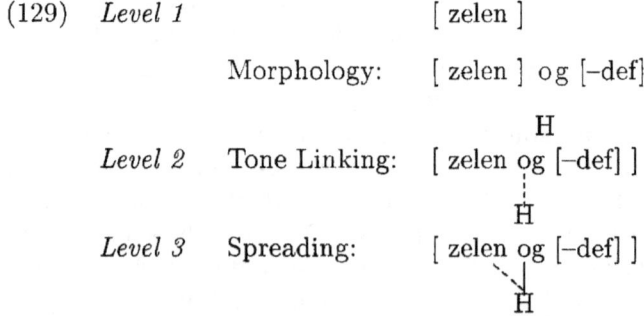

Case Study: Serbo-Croatian

(130)   Level 1:   [zelen]

              Morphology: [zelen [+def]]
                                     H

Cycle 2

    Level 2   Tone Linking: [zelen [+def]]
                                      H

              Morphology: [zelen [+def]] og
                                     H

    Level 3   Spreading: [zelenog [+def]]
                                     H

However, in addition to proposing that the set of default endings is toneless, we will also have to propose that these endings are extrametrical, and therefore incapable of receiving tone. This property has not been obvious so far, since all the stems we looked at have been able to receive tone. But this is not the case with the 'long' stems, which we now turn to.

Recall that, in the case of the nominal oxytone stems (of the productive class), tone would fail to link to the stem's final syllable because it is long. Instead, it would link at the next higher cycle. However, this never happens with the definite adjectival forms of the corresponding class, as illustrated in (131):

(131) a. beela   bêla 'white-def'
         |
        H
   b. beela   béla 'white-indef'
         |
        H

The derivation of the definite class is given in (132), and of the indefinite class in (133):

(132) Level 1   [beel]

              Morphology: [beel [+def]]
                                        H
       Level 2

       Cycle 1   Tone Linking: —

       Cycle 2   Morphology: [b e el [+def]] (og)
                                        H
                 Tone Linking: —

       Level 3

                 Initial High: [beelog [+def]]
                                        ⋮
                                        H

(133) Level 1   [beel]

                 Morphology: [beel] o g [–def]
                                        H
       Level 2   Tone Linking: [beel og [–def]]
                                        ⋮
                                        H
       Level 3   Spreading: [beel og [–def]]
                                        ↘
                                        H

Thus, Tone Linking fails to operate on the definite stem in (132) because the stem final syllable is long. Furthermore, Tone Linking fails to operate on the next higher cycle, as well, because the inflectional ending added at this cycle is invisible. This stem then leaves the cyclic component unlinked to tone, and at Level Three it obtains tone by the postcyclic rule of Initial High Insertion. This motivates a revision of the set of default adjectival endings, as shown in (134):

Case Study: Serbo-Croatian

(134) Default masculine endings (final version):

	Singular	Plural
Nom	(i)	(i)
Acc	(i)/(og)	(e)
Gen	(og)	(ih)
Dat	(om)	(im)
Ins	(im)	(im)
Loc	(om)	(im)

Further support for (134) comes from the behavior of adjectives derived by yer suffixes. In the following section it will be shown that the assumption that Level Two adjectival endings are invisible accounts for a number of their properties.

5.8 Suffixes with Yers

As shown in section 5.3, yer suffixes can appear both at Level One and at Level Two. Furthermore, while Level One yer suffixes trigger presonorant lengthening, Level Two yer suffixes do not. The facts of accent assignment set apart the two classes of yer suffixes as well: those at Level One can never be accented, while those at Level Two can. We will see that the facts of accent assignment corroborate those of presonorant lengthening in that both are accounted for in terms of properties of yers at particular levels.

Let us first examine yer suffixes at Level One. Recall that presonorant lengthening is due to the rule of Yer Delinking, repeated in (135):

(135) Yer Delinking:

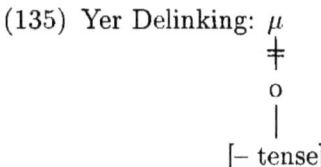

The mora freed by this rule either causes compensatory lengthening (if the preceding consonant is a sonorant), or undergoes stray erasure. We will illustrate this with the Level One suffix -ăn. Examples of forms that have undergone presonorant lengthening are in (136), and of those that have not, in (137).

(136) a. sîlna 'powerful'
b. ŏlōvna 'leaden'

(137) a. kȉšna 'rainy'
b. pšènična 'wheat (adj)'

In both cases, the yer in the stem remains unlinked to the prosodic structure at the first cycle of Level Two, when Tone Linking starts applying. At Level Two, the forms in (136) and (137) undergo two rules, Tonal Node Assignment, which I repeat in (138), and Tone Linking.

(138) Tonal Node Assignment (Level Two): μ_s
$$\vdots$$
$$o$$

The rule in (138) will fail to apply to the yer delinked from the prosodic structure; thus none of the Level One suffixes that begin in a yer will ever be able to be linked to tone. But what is the target of Tone Linking in forms whose final vowel is a delinked yer?

The target of Tone Linking is the immediately preceding syllable. Tone Linking proceeds in its regular fashion, distinguishing between long and short syllables, that is, between those domain-final moras that are linked to a tonal node and those that are not.

The relevant derivations are given in (139). (Tonal nodes are schematically represented with dots underneath vowels; in the actual representation the tonal node and the root node are mediated by a mora.)

Case Study: Serbo-Croatian

(139) Input to Level 2   [oloovăn]   [pšen i čăn]

                                            H   H
        Tonal Node Assign: [o̥lo̥ovăn]   [pšę̊n i̥ čăn]

                                            H   H
        Tone Linking: —   [pšę̊n i̥ čăn]

                                                                        H
        Morphology: [o̥lo̥ovăn] (a)   [pšę̊ničăn] (a)
                                           H   H̥
        Tone Linking: —   —

    Level 3

        Initial High: [o̥lo̥ovňa]   —
                                            H̥

The form *pšeničan*, whose pre-yer syllable is short, will obtain tone by virtue of Tone Linking. In contrast, Tone Linking fails to operate on *oloovan* because the syllable preceding the yer suffix contains a long vowel, due to presonorant lengthening; on the next higher cycle, Tone Linking again fails because the adjectival inflectional ending is invisible. Thus the only remaining source of tone is the Initial High Insertion, as shown by the derivation in (139).

Note that stems whose pre-yer syllable contains an underlying long vowel, for example *jŭnaačna*, behave exactly like *őloovna*. Although the form *junaak* has its own tone, this tone fails to be linked by the cyclic rule in the form *jŭnaačna* for the same reason it fails to be linked to it *őloovna* — first it cannot link to the syllable with a long vowel, and second, it cannot link to the invisible inflection. The Initial High Insertion then remains its only source of tone.

This gives us two relevant classes of stems affiliated with tone: those in which the syllable preceding the suffix has a short vowel, and those in which this syllable has a long vowel. While the former class obtains tone on the pre-yer syllable, the latter class never does, due to the mode of operation of Tone Linking.

The situation with yer suffixes at Level Two is somewhat different. The yers in the suffix also undergo Yer Delinking, just like those at Level One. But unlike the Level One yer suffixes, the ones at Level Two can be linked to tone. This suggests the ordering of the relevant rules as in (140):

(140) Rule ordering at Level Two:
Tonal Node Assignment
Tone Linking
Yer Delinking

In other words, yers that belong to Level Two suffixes will be linked to tone before the application of Yer Delinking. The question arises what happens with the tone linked to a yer after this segment is delinked from the structure, as in (141):

(141) a. [čovek ă]
        ǂ
        H

b. [junaak ă]
        ǂ
        H

c. [cirkus ăsk-]
        ǂ
        H

d. [junaak ăsk-]
        ǂ
        H

I propose that tone on the delinked yer is relinked to the closest tonal node, which is always the one on the preceding syllable, since all these processes are cyclic. The rule responsible for this will be a tone relinking rule, which I refer to here as Metatony, following traditional terminology. Once the yer is delinked from its mora, the mora itself will delink both from the syllable node and from the tonal node assigned to it. This will cause the relinking of tone from the 'floating' tonal node to the next one available, which will always be to the left.

(142) Metatony: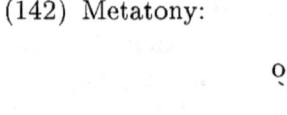

Case Study: Serbo-Croatian

But this brings us to an interesting prediction. Recall that for the purposes of Tone Linking, we had to assume that, at Level Two, tonal nodes are assigned only to the strong moras, that is, to those that act as syllable heads. This predicts that the relinking process will also assign tone only to the head mora of the previous syllable, since these will be the only moras associated with tonal nodes. This is precisely what happens, as shown by the output of Metatony in (143):

(143)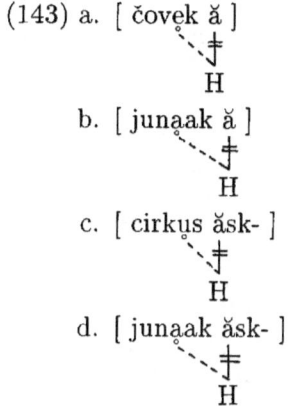
a. [čovek ă]

b. [junaak ă]

c. [cirkus ăsk-]

d. [junaak ăsk-]

Thus, unlike Level One yer suffixes, those at Level Two can be preceded by tone regardless of the vowel length in the preceding syllable. To illustrate this, let us look at the derivations of *jùnāčki* and *jȕnāčna*:

(144) Level 1   [junaak]   [junaak]
                                      H   H
       Morphology: [junaak ăn]   —

       Yer Delinking: [junaak ăn]   —

       Level 2

       Tonal Node Assign: [jy̦na̦ak ăn]   [jy̦na̦ak]
                                      H   H
       Tone Linking: —   —

       Morphology: —   [jy̦na̦ak ăsk]
                                                      H
       Tonal Node Assign: —   [jy̦na̦ak ă̦sk]
                                                      H
       Tone Linking: —   [jy̦na̦ak ă̦sk]
                                                          |
                                                          Ḣ
       Yer Delinking: —   [jy̦na̦akă̦sk]
                                                          |
                                                          Ḣ
       Metatony: —   [jy̦na̦akă̦sk]
                                                          |
                                                          Ḣ
       Level 3

       Initial High: junaačna   —
                                  |
                                  Ḣ

To summarize, Level One yers can be preceded by a syllable linked to tone only if this syllable contains a short vowel. In contrast, a Level Two yer can be preceded by a syllable linked to tone regardless of the vowel length that it contains. Thus, the linking status of the yers at the two cyclic levels accounts both for presonorant lengthening and for the facts of tone assignment.

Case Study: Serbo-Croatian   171

5.9 Verbal Forms

The coverage of Tone Linking is quite broad; in addition to the nominal and adjectival forms, this rule also accounts for the accent of verbal forms. To show this, I must first analyze the basic facts about verbal morphology.

Verbs are divided into the so-called thematic and athematic class, that is, into those that possess a theme vowel and those that do not. Only the former class will be dealt with here; the latter class is unproductive and consists of a small group of verbs, many of which have clear Indo-European counterparts. According to the traditional view, a verbal form of the thematic class consists of a root, a theme vowel, and the inflectional ending, as shown in (145):

(145) vol   e   ti   voleti 'love(Inf)'
       root   theme   inflection

Verbs from the thematic class are further subdivided into three classes, depending on whether they select the *a*, *e*, or *i* theme vowel. For example, the verb *pevati* 'sing' subcategorizes for the *a* theme, the verb *voleti* 'love' for the *e* theme, and the verb *misliti* 'think' for the *i* theme.

(146) Theme Vowels

a	pev-a-ti	pevati 'sing(Inf)'
e	vol-e-ti	voleti 'love(Inf)'
i	misl-i-ti	misliti 'think(Inf)'

Given the separation of the lexicon into three levels proposed for Serbo-Croatian in this chapter, the most natural analysis of these forms is to assign the theme vowel to Level One and the inflections to Level Two. Thus, Level One contains the three theme 'allophones', and individual verbs subcategorize for one of them:

(147) Level One: *a, e, i*

The forms in (146), being in the infinitive, are derived from the so-called 'infinitival stem'. The preterite forms also derive from the 'infinitival stem', as shown by the following:

(148) a. pev-a-la pevala 'sang(Fem)'
   b. vol-e-la volela 'loved(Fem)'
   c. misl-i-la mislila 'thought(Fem)'

The forms that can be traced back to the 'infinitival stem' present a relatively straightforward picture of how the verb is divided into the root, the theme, and the ending. The other class of forms, those that derive from the so-called 'present tense stem', are somewhat more complex. In (149) are listed the first person present tense forms corresponding to those in (148):

(149) a. pevam '(I) sing (Pres.)'
   b. volim '(I) love (Pres.)'
   c. mislim '(I) think (Pres.)'

In (149)b the ending is obviously -im; I will propose that all endings pattern with that of (149)b, and that the stems should be parsed as shown in (150):

(150) a. pev-am
   b. vol-im
   c. misl-im

But we may wonder what has happened with the theme vowel which, as claimed earlier, is a regular part of the verbal form. My claim will be that the theme vowel is indeed present at a more abstract level of the representation, that is, that the forms in (150) are derived from those in (151):

(151) a. pev-a-am
   b. vol-e-im
   c. misl-i-im

To account for the cases in Russian comparable to those in (151), Lightner 1972 proposes the rule of Stem Truncation, given in (152):

(152) $V \rightarrow \emptyset\ /\ \_\_\_ V$

I will adopt this rule to account for the 'present tense stems'.

Case Study: Serbo-Croatian

This rule operates at Level Two; the following derivation shows how it accounts for the forms in (150):[32]

(153) Level 2

	peva	vole	misli
Morphology	peva-am	vole-im	misli-im
Stem Truncation	pevam	volim	mislim

Thus, the traditional division into the 'present tense' and 'infinitival' stems can be attributed to the Stem Truncation Rule: it applies in the former, but not in the latter case. This analysis gains further support from the distribution of accent, which we now turn to.

Taking the morphological structure of the verbal form as our point of departure, we can say that verbs fall into three accentual classes: those which have accent on the stem, those whose accent is on the theme vowel, and those with alternating accent.

We will start with forms whose accent alternates between the stem and the theme vowel; with the infinitival forms the accent is on the theme, and with the present tense forms it is on the stem. This is illustrated by two a theme verbs, ìgrati 'dance' and spávati 'sleep'; the former has a short stem vowel, and the latter's stem vowel is long.

(154) Present Tense Forms

ȉgram '(I) dance'	ȉgramo '(we) dance'
ȉgraš '(you) dance'	ȉgrate '(you) dance'
ȉgra '(he/she) dances'	ȉgraju '(they) dance'

(155) Past Tense Forms
    igrati   dance(Inf)
    igrao(M), igrala(F), igralo(N)   dance(PastPart, Sg)
    igrali(M), igrale(F), igrala(N)   dance(PastPart, Pl)

(156) Present Tense Forms

spâvam '(I) sleep	spâvamo '(we) sleep
spâvaš '(you) sleep	spâvate '(you) sleep
spâva '(he/she) sleeps'	spàvaju '(they) sleep'

(157) Past Tense Forms
spávati   sleep(Inf)
spávao(M), spávala(F), spávalo(N)   sleep(PastPart, Sg)
spávali(M), spávale(F), spávala(N)   sleep(PastPart, Pl)

This accentual class is highly productive; the alternating pattern is found among all thematic verbal forms, regardless of the particular theme vowel they are associated with, as shown by the following examples with the *e* and *i* themes respectively:

(158) vòleti 'love(Inf) *vs.* vőlim '(I) love (Pres)'

(159) a. mòliti 'plead(Inf) *vs.* mŏlim '(I) plead (Pres)'
      b. ráditi 'work(Inf) *vs.* râdim '(I) work (Pres)'

It will now be shown that this accentual pattern is due to the rule of Stem Truncation. Let us assume that the alternating verbal forms are all affiliated with tone. Next, recall that the theme vowel is located at Level One, and that Tone Linking applies at Level Two. Under these assumptions, the derivation of the infinitival forms with the *a* theme will be quite simple, as shown in (160):

(160) *Level 1*   igr   spaav

                                    H   H
              Morphology: igr a   spaav a

                                    H   H
      Level 2 Tone Linking: igra   spaava
                                    | |
                                    H   H
              Morphology: igra ti   spaava ti
                                    | |
                                    H   H
      Level 3 Spreading: igra ti   spaava ti
                                    ↘   ↘
                                    H   H

Present tense forms are less straightforward, since in this case two other rules apply as well, Stem Truncation and Metatony introduced in section 5.8. The rule of Metatony is of particular relevance in those cases when the vowel deleted by Stem Trunca-

Case Study: Serbo-Croatian

tion is linked to tone. In this case, tone also gets delinked, and then relinks to the first available tonal node, which will always be to the left.

(161)   Level 1

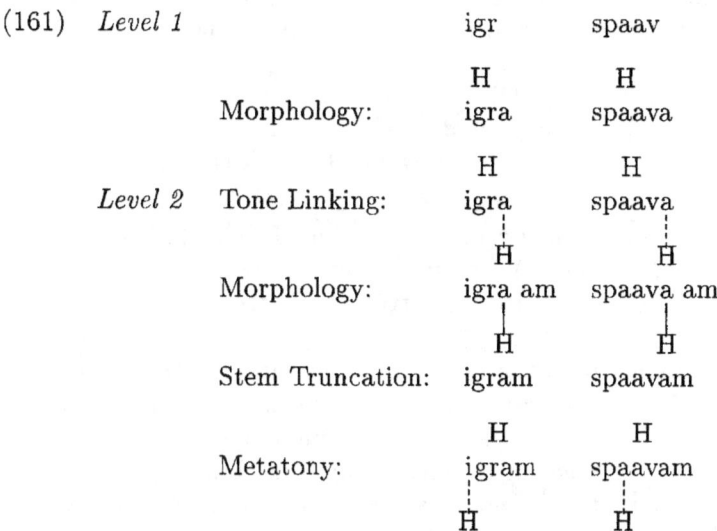

Note that in *spaavam* tone is assigned to a syllable containing a long vowel; the only cyclic rule that can assign tone to a long vowel is Metatony, which further supports the analysis proposed here.

Finally, we need to comment on the fact that the third person present tense forms of some of the verbs that belong to the alternating class share the accentual pattern with the infinitive, as shown in (154) and (157), and repeated in (162):

(162) a. igraju ìgraju
       |
       H
    b. spaavaju spávaju
       |
       H

This is due to the failure of Stem Truncation to apply in this context. The inflectional ending is in this case *-ju*; since this ending does not begin in a vowel, the preceding theme is not deleted, and the accent remains on the theme.

We are left with two more accentual classes, one containing verbal forms with the accent on the stem, as in (163), and the other consisting of those whose accent is on the theme, as in (164).

(163) a. pȅvati 'sing(Inf)'   pȅvam '(I) sing (Pres)'
   b. vȉdeti 'see(Inf)'   vȉdim '(I) see (Pres)'
   c. mȉsliti 'think(Inf)'   mȉslim '(I) think (Pres)'

(164) a. zvíždati 'whistle(Inf)'   zvíždim '(I) whistle (Pres)'
   b. žíveti 'live(Inf)'   žívim '(I) live (Pres)'
   c. trúbiti 'trumpit(Inf)'   trúbim '(I) trumpet (Pres)'

Let us start with the class whose accent is on the stem. This again is a fairly productive group. Furthermore, it consists almost exclusively of verbs with a short stem final vowel, which strongly suggests that the accent is assigned by Tone Linking rather than by some other rule.[33] But how does tone get to the stem vowel, if the final vowel of the form that arrives at Level Two normally belongs to the theme?

It appears in fact that, with these forms, the theme vowel is invisible at the point at which Tone Linking applies. However, the theme vowel does not have this property with other accentual classes. One solution might be to posit two series of themes — the visible and the invisible ones — and to associate them with different verbal classes. Another solution is to mark this particular class as triggering a rule which makes the theme vowel invisible. I will adopt here the latter solution, whose advantage is that it allows us to retain a single class of theme vowels.

If we adopt the invisibility of the theme, Tone Linking will only be able to assign tone to a stem mora, as shown by the following derivations:

Case Study: Serbo-Croatian

(165)   Level 1   pev   pev

                                             H   H
                 Morphology: pev a   pev a

                                             H   H
                 Invisibility: pev (a)   pev (a)

                                             H   H
        Level 2 Tone Linking: pev(a)   pev(a)
                                             | |
                                             H́   H́

                 Morphology: peva ti   peva am
                                             | |
                                             H́   H́

                 Stem Truncation: —   pevam
                                                        |
                                                        H́

Note that our further prediction is that, if this class contains any long stems, those will not have accent on the stem. As I will presently show, the verbs in (164) whose accent is on the theme have exactly the same properties as those in (163). The accentual difference results from the difference in vowel length, which Tone Linking is sensitive to. Note that with the additional assumption that the infinitival ending is also extrametrical, the derivations of forms in (164) are practically identical to the derivations of forms in (163). In other words, (166) parallels (165):

		truub	truub
Level 1			
		H	H
	Morphology:	truub i	truub i
		H	H
	Invisibility:	truub (i)	truub (i)
(166)			H	H
Level 2	Tone Linking:	—	—
	Morphology:	truubi (ti)	truubi im
		H	H
	Stem Truncation:	—	truubim
			H

Finally, short stems with accent on the theme, such as those in (167), can be thought of as being toneless. If we further assume that the theme vowel is affiliated with tone, we get exactly the result we need.

(167) a. čìtati 'read(Inf)' čìtam '(I) read(Pres)'
    b. tr̀peti 'suffer(Inf)' tr̀pim '(I) suffer (Pres)'

5.10 Concluding Remarks

A most striking consequence of this analysis is that dominance can be viewed as resulting from interactions between tone linking and level ordering. As we have seen, throughout the cyclic component of the grammar tone can be linked only to a short syllable. This, combined with level ordering, accounts for most of the accentual behavior found both with simple and with derived stems. First, we account for the fact that all accented stems ending in a long vowel, both simple and derived, exhibit a post-accenting behavior. Second, we account for the dominant vs. recessive behavior of individual suffixes. These phenomena have been dealt with in the literature by invoking special mechanisms — for example, by marking individual suffixes as stress deleting, or by associating the dominant vs. recessive behavior of suffixes with properties of particular levels (see Halle and Mohanan 1985, Halle and Vergnaud 1987, Poser 1984b). But here, nothing special needs to be said about any of the accentual properties we find either in the lexicon or in the organization of the levels. All these properties follow solely from the operation of the Tone Linking Rule.

Earlier approaches have associated dominance with structure-changing processes. Mine is an attempt to handle dominance in a structure-building fashion. Under this constrained approach the strategy is to identify the point at which a certain type of structure, for example tone, is assigned to forms. The alternative assumption, that most of the structure is present from the earliest points of the derivation and then lost on the way, may obliterate a number of regularities and lead to loss of generalization.

Notes

[1] The question arises, of course, why syllabification is deferred until Level Two. We could assume a filter against syllable structure which is operative at Level One, in accordance with the Strong Domain Hypothesis, and then gets turned off at Level Two. A direct consequence of this is that neither syllabification nor any of the rules dependent on syllable structure will be able to apply at Level One, although they may well be present at this level.

[2] The only source of hiatus between like vowels is if identical heteromorphemic vowels happen to be adjacent, as in *po-oštriti* 'sharpen', where the prefix ends, and the stem begins in *o*. Hiatus between unlike vowels occurs morpheme internally, as well as across morpheme boundaries.

[3] In addition to cyclic presonorant lengthening, we also find the postcyclic version of this process, which applies at Level Three.

[4] Halle's is an account of the Čakavian dialect of Serbo-Croatian, while the present chapter is based on the data from a Štokavian dialect. However, the yer facts are the same in the Čakavian and Štokavian; in both cases the yer is vocalized as *a*.

[5] In the literature, the vowel *a* is classified as back (Belić 1956).

[6] The palatalization pattern triggered by *i* is quite regular, unlike that exhibited by the other palatalizing vowels.

[7] An alternative might be to posit a floating feature in the representation of palatalizing suffixes. However, this would leave unexplained the fact that only suffixes beginning in a front vowel happen to be associated with such a feature.

[8] This rule is commonly construed as a rule of lowering rather than laxing (Lightner 1972, Gussman 1980, Rubach 1984). However, given the facts presented here, it would be difficult to justify a lowering process.

[9] In the examples below, as well as throughout this chapter, Serbo-Croatian long vowels will be represented as geminates. All the cases we deal with will the cases of tautosyllabic geminated vowels; heterosyllabic geminated vowels, which do appear in Serbo-Croatian (see note 2) are outside the scope of this analysis. This is a departure from the standard orthography, which makes no vowel length distinctions.

[10] On strict cyclicity see Rubach 1984 and the references therein.

[11] The account of compensatory lengthening in terms of filling

a vacated subsyllabic position is originally due to Ingria 1980. See also Steriade 1982.

[12] On Japanese suffixes with comparable properties, see Poser 1984a, 1984b, 1990.

[13] This is not the only suffix that forms comparatives; this particular one is associated with only a restricted class of adjectives, while the other one, the suffix *-ij*, is used as an elsewhere form.

[14] For arguments why this rule applies right to left rather than left to right, see Inkelas and Zec 1988.

[15] Stress will appear on the final syllable of those polysyllabic words which are exceptions to Spreading, for example in *asistȇnt* 'assistant'. Exceptions to Spreading are found among words with High linked to the nonfinal syllable as well, as in *verovȃtno* 'possibly'.

[16] In the account of Inkelas and Zec they are prelinked, since their location in a word is taken to be unpredictable. We will see in a moment that this is an overly pessimistic view.

[17] Pulleyblank 1983, 1986 argues that tonal rules, just like any other rules, can be either lexical or postlexical.

[18] This property was observed by Leskien 1975, who gave the following rules for the accent of derived forms (note in particular the b. clause):

a. Alte Länge der Suffixsilbe bleibt erhalten unmittelbar vor der (ursprünglichen) Hochtonsilbe des Wortes.

b. Alte Länge der Suffixsilbe wird verkürzt, wenn diese Silbe selbst den (ursprünglichen) Hochton trägt. Länge in einer (ursprünglich) betonten Suffixsilbe kommt nicht vor.

c. Alte Länge der Suffixsilbe bleibt erhalten nach der (ursprünglichen) Hochtonsilbe des Wortes.

I will claim that the incompatibility of tone and length is not limited only to derived environments.

[19] For the interpretation of the accent marks see 145. The macron over a vowel indicates toneless length

[20] The genitive plural form regularly has a falling rather than a rising accent. I will assume that this difference is caused by the fact that the genitive plural ending lengthens the vowel in the preceding syllable. Note that the tone in *bundev-* is linked to the second syllable before the genitive ending is added. Once it is added, the syllable that has tone linked its only mora gets lengthened; if we assume that vowel lengthening consists in adding the head mora (accompanied by relabeling), then tone will end up on a nonhead

mora, and will have to be delinked. It will be linked to the next mora to the left that possesses the tonal node, and this mora will be in the immediately preceding syllable.

[21] Note that the masculine singular form has a different accent. This is due to the fact that the ending in this case is a yer.

[22] The tonal nodes are not represented in this or any other derivation to be given here. The vocalic segments in all the forms are moraic, and if they are also syllable heads, they will be associated with a tonal node.

[23] Crucially, the inflectional suffix ends in a short syllable; if it ended in a long syllable, tone linking would again have to be blocked.

[24] Some 'short' stems belong to the oxytone class as well, as will be shown in a moment.

[25] The singular accusative ending has two allomorphs: -a is added to animate, and ă to inanimate forms. The two allomorphs of the singular locative form have the same distribution: the accented form is added to the inanimate stems, and the unaccented form to the animate stems.

[26] The suffix - at has templatic properties, as shown in section 5.3.

[27] The long vowel of the stem is shortened, due to the general process whereby preaccentual length is lost.

[28] The exception that I have no account for is vâtren 'fiery'; this stem should be treated as affiliated with tone for other purposes, but in this case it behaves as if it were toneless.

[29] Another suffix of the -aad class is -iišt. Again I have not been able to find any forms that exhibit what we predict to be the oxytone properties.

[30] The nominative singular form of the indefinite paradigm also has accent on the ending, although this is not obvious from its surface form. The ending of this form is a yer vowel, as shown in (169); tone is linked to the yer vowel, which subsequently undergoes Yer Delinking. This then causes the relinking of tone to the closest mora on the left, which in this case belongs to the stem. We discuss this process in more detail in section 5.8.

[31] Forms with these suffixes are also discussed in section 5.3.

[32] In a number of cases, the theme vowel has the same form as the initial vowel of the present tense inflection. I have no account for this coincidence.

[33] Daničić lists forms like pâmtiti 'remember', trâmpiti 'barter',

Case Study: Serbo-Croatian

kȉcošiti (se) 'make (oneself) elegant', *kârtati (se)* 'play cards' etc., which have accent on a stem syllable which contains a long vowel. The class of such verbs is very small — about twenty altogether — and they can be dealt with by prelinking.

6

Consequences for Prosodic Phonology

In this study I have made two general claims. First, I have argued for the mora as a subsyllabic constituent, that is, for the representation of subsyllabic structure as in (1):

(1)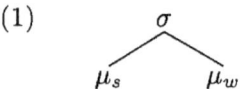

Second, I have argued that the mora is a prosodic constituent occupying the lowest position in the prosodic hierarchy.

Arguments for the prosodic status of the mora advanced in Chapter Four have been based on its ability to provide prosodic licensing at those points of the derivation at which syllables have not yet been created (if the creation of these two prosodic constituents happens not to be simultaneous). In this chapter I will show that the mora behaves like a prosodic constituent in several other respects as well.

First, moras can be invisible to rules, that is, they can be extrametrical. According to Poser 1984b (and the references therein), accented verb stems in Japanese obtain accent on the syllable containing the penultimate mora:

(2) a. kake'ru 'hang'
     b. ka'u   'raise (an animal)'
     c. suku'u 'build a nest'
     d. ue'ru   'starve'

A simple account of these facts, according to Poser, is first, to assume that accent is assigned to moras; and second, that the stem-final mora is extrametrical for the purposes of accent assignment. Under these assumptions, accent is assigned to the final visible mora of the stem, which accounts for the pattern in (2). From our perspective, this case is of particular interest because syllables containing short vowels, as in (2)a,d pattern with the second half of a long vowel (2)c, or of a diphthong (2)b, which presents a good argument in favor of positing moras as subsyllabic, as well as prosodic, constituents. This brings moras on a par with syllables, which may be extrametrical to the rules of stress assignment.

A further prediction of the present claim is that moras can form reduplicative templates, just like the syllable (and the foot). I have not found any cases of such reduplicative templates, and it remains to be seen what evidence can be found in support of this hypothesis.

Let us now turn to the prosodic hierarchy itself, and see what is gained by adding the mora as its lowest constituent. In Chapter Four, I proposed to expand the prosodic hierarchy, as shown in (3):

(3) Prosodic Hierarchy
    phonological phrase
    phonological word
    foot
    syllable
    mora

An important point about this hierarchy is that it does not rest on a unifying property shared by all its constituent parts. This view has been expressed in Selkirk 1986 and Inkelas 1989. Selkirk 1986:385 observes that the higher constituents in the hierarchy differ from the lower ones in their mode of generation. Constituents like the phonological word and the phonological phrase are generated by a mapping into the morphosyntactic structure, which is not the case with the lower down constituents. This, according to Selkirk, creates a 'discontinuity' in the hierarchy; as a remedy, she proposes to exclude from the hierarchy all constituents lower than the phonological word, and to keep only those constituents which are systematically mapped into the morphosyntactic structure. Selkirk's revised version of the prosodic hierarchy corresponds to (4):

(4)   Revised Prosodic Hierarchy (Selkirk 1986)
      phonological phrase
      phonological word

Selkirk further claims that this move is in fact necessary if we want to retain the Strict Layer Hypothesis, repeated in (5).

(5)   *Strict Layer Hypothesis:* A category of level i in the hierarchy immediately dominates (a sequence of) categories at level $i - 1$. [Selkirk 1984b]

In particular, prosodic constituents such as the phonological word or the phonological phrase may serve as domains of foot construction. Thus, a constituent at level i makes reference directly to a constituent at level $i-2$, which violates the intrinsic locality of the Strict Layer Hypothesis. We can add a few more violations of this sort. As we saw in Chapter Four, the domain of syllabification in Bulgarian is the phonological word; in this case, a unit at level i has actually been created by phonological rules before a unit at level $i-2$. Furthermore, constraints on the minimal size imposed on words, arguably phonological words, are often expressed in terms of moras, rather than syllables, as would be required by the Strict Layer Hypothesis (see McCarthy and Prince 1986). Implicit in Selkirk's claim is that the constituents that remain in the prosodic hierarchy, that is, the phonological word and the phonological phrase, are always strictly layered and never give rise to violations of the sort just described. However, Selkirk does not address the issue of whether the constituents left out of the hierarchy exhibit the property of strict layering, that is, whether they should continue their existence independently of each other or form a hierarchy of their own.

The latter solution is proposed in Inkelas (forthcoming). Inkelas in fact posits two hierarchies, one morphosyntactic, and one metrical. The hierarchy in (4), which I repeat in (6), is the Morphosyntactically Based Hierarchy:

(6) Morphosyntactically Based Hierarchy
     phonological phrase
     phonological word

I will now focus on what Inkelas terms the metrical hierarchy. My proposal consists in taking sonority to be the defining property of the prosodic hierarchy containing the residual constituents.

(7) Sonority-Based Prosodic Hierarchy
     foot
     syllable
     mora

My claim will be that, what the mora, the syllable, and the foot have in common is being constrained in terms of sonority. This property is not shared by any higher up units, those whose membership in a hierarchy is based on morphosyntactic mappings. Moreover, I will claim that it is by virtue of including the mora into the hierarchy that we will be able to identify sonority as its unifying feature.

As we have seen, both moras and syllables are constrained with respect to sonority; we have also seen that the head relation assigned to the s-labeled subconstituent serves as a path for sonority constraints on the syllable to percolate to the head mora.

(8)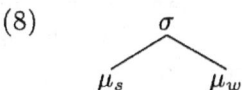

The question arises whether this relation between the mora and the syllable also extends to the foot. While no one has proposed sonority constraints on feet, certain constraints that have been proposed are restatable in those terms. It has been noted that certain types of syllabic segments cannot appear in the stressed syllable; this covers both syllabic consonants and vowels of the schwa class, that is, those that are lax. Furthermore, the stressed syllable is the only position in foot structure in which the occurrence of syllabic segments is not free.

This is highly reminiscent of what we saw to be the sonority relation between syllables and moras. Recall that the set of segments that can license a syllable is a subset of those that can license a mora. We can extend this by saying that the set of segments that can license a foot is a subset of those that can license a syllable. Under this assumption, we can expect to find a situation in which only a subset of syllabic segments can head the strong syllable of a foot. If this happens to be a proper subset, then the syllabic segments excluded from this position will be the least sonorous ones.

Note that we can express this by the mechanism that captures this same relation between the syllable and the mora. The basic structure we get is as in (9):

(9)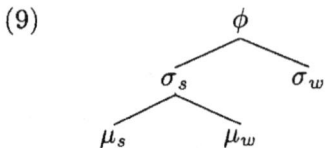

If the constraints imposed at the level of the foot are constraints on sonority, they can percolate down to the head syllable, and thus further constrain the sonority requirements on the syllable; and then percolate further to the head mora. Again, the percolation path consists of s-labeled categories. Note that this again derives a subset relation between the sonority constraints on the foot and those on the syllable.

Let us now look at the kinds of constraints that have been imposed on the stressed syllable. In English, for example, syllabic consonants never obtain stress. This is in keeping with our claim that the foot may also impose sonority constraints: note that again, the syllabic segments excluded from the stressed position are the least sonorous ones. Another case that deserves to be mentioned in this context is Eastern Cheremis (Hayes 1981). In this language stress assignment is sensitive to the full/reduced vowel distinction: Stress is assigned to the last full vowel of a word if there is one, otherwise to the initial vowel. We could characterize this system by saying that the basic foot is constrained by sonority in that it can only be headed by a nonlax vowel; if a word has no nonlax vowels foot structure will simply not be built. The word tree, however, is not constrained in this fashion, and it is by virtue of the word tree that a word containing only lax vowels gets stress.

An important consequence of adopting the mora as a prosodic unit is that we obtain a simple and unified characterization of constituent weight. If we assume that prosodic structure is generally the locus of weight structure, then each prosodic unit can minimally contain only one immediately lower prosodic unit and be light, or more than one, and be heavy. If so, we expect that the lowest unit would be indivisible into further prosodic units and will therefore exhibit no heaviness effects. Such a unit cannot be the syllable; only mora is eligible for this status.

Our characterization of constituent weight makes reference to tree geometry, in accordance with Hayes' 1981 claim:

(10)   A prosodic constituent is heavy if and only if it has branching structure.

In the case of the syllable, there is no need to identify a subsyllabic node relevant for this characterization, since all the information is contained right underneath the syllable node itself. In other words, all nonsimplex prosodic units can have branching structure, which is interpreted exclusively as branching into units at the next lower level. The facts about prosodic weight thus independently argue for a subsyllabic level of prosodic structure with moras as its units.

Bibliography

Aronson, H. 1968. *Bulgarian Inflectional Morphophonology.* Slavistic Printings and Reprintings, 70. The Hague: Mouton.

Augustaitis, D.L. 1964. *Das litauische Phonationssystem.* München: Verlag Otto Sagner.

Bach, E. 1978. "Long Vowels and Stress in Kwakiutl." Unpublished manuscript, University of Massachusetts at Amherst.

Basbøll, H. 1985. "Stød in Modern Danish." *Folia Linguistica* 19:1-50.

Belić, A. 1956. *Fonetika.* Beograd: Naučna knjiga.

Boas, F. 1947. "Kwakiutl Grammar with a Glossary of the Suffixes." *Transactions of the American Philosophical Society.* New Series, Vol. 37, Part 3, Philadelphia.

Booij, G. and J. Rubach. 1984. "Morphological and Prosodic Domains in Lexical Phonology." *Phonology Yearbook* 1:1-29.

Booij, G. and J. Rubach. 1987. "Postcyclic versus Postlexical Rules in Lexical Phonology." *Linguistic Inquiry* 18:1-44.

Browne, E.W. and J. McCawley. 1965. "Srpskohrvatski akcenat." *Zbornik za filologiju i lingvistiku* 8:147-151.

Chierchia, G. 1982. "An Autosegmental Theory of Raddoppiamento." In Pustejovsky, J. and P. Sells (eds.), *Proceedings of the Twelfth Annual Meeting of the North Eastern Linguistic Society,* 49-62. University of Massachussetts, Amherst.

Chomsky, N. and M. Halle. 1968. *Sound Pattern of English*. New York: Harper and Row.

Clements, G. N. 1985. "The Geometry of Phonological Features." *Phonology Yearbook* 2:225-254.

Clements, G. N. 1990. "The Role of the Sonority Cycle in Core Syllabification." In Kingston, J. and M. Beckman (eds.) *Laboratory Phonology I*. Cambridge University Press.

Clements, G. N. and S. J. Keyser. 1983. *CV Phonology. A Generative Theory of the Syllable*. Cambridge (Mass.): The MIT Press.

Daničić, Dj. 1925. *Srpski akcenti*. Beograd-Zemun: Srpska Kraljevska Akademija.

de Chene, B. and S. Anderson. 1979. "Compensatory Lengthening." *Language* 55:505-535.

Dell, F. and M. Elmedlaoui. 1985. "Syllabic Consonants and Syllabification in Imdlawn Tashlhiyt Berber." *Journal of African Languages and Linguistics* 7:105-130.

Elson, M. J. 1976. "The Definite Article in Bulgarian and Macedonian." *SEEJ* 20:273-279.

Fischer-Jørgensen, E. 1985. "Stød in Standard Danish." *Annual Report of the Institute of Phonetics, University of Copenhagen* 19.

Gazdar, G. and G. K. Pullum. 1982. *Generalized Phrase Structure Grammar: A Theoretical Synopsis*. Bloomington: Indiana University Linguistics Club.

Gazdar, G., E. Klein, G.K. Pullum, and I. Sag. 1985. *Generalized Phrase Structure Grammar*. Cambridge (Mass.): Harvard University Press.

Grubb, D. M. 1977. *A Practical Writing System and Short Dictionary of Kwakw'ala (Kwakiutl)*. Ottawa: National Museums of Canada.

Gussman, E. 1980. *Studies in Abstract Phonology*. Cambridge (Mass.): The MIT Press

Halle, M. 1971. "Remarks on Slavic Accentology." *Linguistic Inquiry* 2:1-19.

Halle, M. 1979. "The Accentual System of the Serbo-Croatian Dialect of Novi." Unpublished manuscript, MIT.

Halle, M. and P. Kiparsky. 1981. Review of *Histoire de l'accentuation slave* by Paul Garde. *Language* 57:150-181.

Halle, M. and K.P. Mohanan. 1985. "Segmental Phonology of Modern English." *Linguistic Inquiry* 16:57-116.

Halle, M. and J.-R. Vergnaud. 1987. "Stress and the Cycle." *Linguistic Inquiry* 18:45-84.

Hankamer, J. and J. Aissen. 1974. "The Sonority Hierarchy." In Bruck et al. (eds.) *Papers from the Parasession on Natural Phonology*. Chicago: Chicago Linguistic Society.

Hayes, B. 1981. *A Metrical Theory of Stress Rules*. Doctoral Dissertation, Massachusetts Institute of Technology. Reproduced by the Indiana Linguistics Club. Bloomington, Indiana.

Hayes, B. 1982. "Metrical Structure as the Organizing Principle of Yidin^y Phonology." In van der Hulst, H. and N. Smith (eds.) *The Structure of Phonological Representation*. Part I. Dordrecht: Foris Publications.

Hayes, B. 1986. "Inalterability in CV Phonology." *Language* 62:321- 351.

Hayes, B. 1989a. "The Prosodic Hierarchy and Meter." In Kiparsky, P. and G. Youmans, eds., *Rhythm and Meter*, 201-260. Academic Press: Orlando.

Hayes, B. 1989b. "Compensatory Lengthening in Moraic Phonology." *Linguistic Inquiry* 20: 253-306.

Hayes, B. 1993. *Metrical Stress Theory. Principles and Case Studies*. Unpublished manuscript, UCLA.

Hoard, J. E. 1978. "Remarks on the Nature of Syllabic Stops and Affricates." In Bell, A. and J. B. Hooper (eds.). *Syllables and Segments*. Amsterdam: North Holland Publishing Company.

Hooper, J. B. 1972. "The Syllable in Phonological Theory." *Language* 48:525:40.

Hooper, J. B. 1976. *An Introduction to Generative Natural Phonology*. New York: Academic Press.

Hyman, L. 1985. *A Theory of Phonological Weight*. Dordrecht: Foris Publications.

Illich-Svitych, V. M. 1979. *Nominal Accentuation in Baltic and Slavic*. Cambridge (Mass.): The MIT Press.

Ingria, R. 1980. "Compensatory Lengthening as a Metrical Phenomenon." *Linguistic Inquiry* 11:465-495.

Inkelas, S. 1987. "Prosodic Dependence in the Lexicon." Paper presented at the 62nd Meeting of the Linguistic Society of America, San Francisco, CA.

Inkelas, S. 1988a. "Tone Feature Geometry." In Blevins, J. and J. Carter (eds.), *Proceedings of the Eighteenth Annual Meeting of the North Eastern Linguistic Society*, Vol. 1:223-237. University of Massachusetts, Amherst.

Inkelas, S. 1988b. "Prosodic Constraints on Syntax: Hausa 'fa'." In H. Borer (ed.), *Proceedings of the Seventh West Coast Conference on Formal Linguistics*, 375-389.. Stanford Linguistics Association.

Inkelas, S. 1989. *Prosodic Constituency in the Lexicon*. Doctoral Dissertation. Stanford University.

Inkelas, S. and D. Zec. 1988. "Serbo-Croatian Pitch Accent: The Interactions of Tone, Stress, and Intonation." *Language* 64:227- 248.

Itô, J. 1986. *Syllable Theory in Prosodic Phonology*. Doctoral Dissertation. University of Massachusetts.

Itô, J. 1989. "A Prosodic Theory of Epenthesis." *Natural Language and Linguistic Theory* 7:217-259.

Ivić, P. 1965. "Prozodijski sistem savremenog srpskohrvatskog standardnog jezika." *Symbolae linguisticae in honorem Georgii Kurylowicz*, 133-44. Wroclaw, Warsaw, and Cracow.

Ivić, P. 1976. "Serbocroatian Accentuation: Facts and Interpretation." In Magner, T.F. (ed.) *Slavic Linguistics and Language Teaching,* 34-43. Cambridge (Mass.): Slavica.

Jakobson, R. 1962 [1937] . "On the Identification of Phonemic Entities." *Selected Writings I*, 418-425. The Hague: Mouton.

Kahn, D. 1976. *Syllable-Based Generalizations in English Phonology.* Doctoral Dissertation. Massachusetts Institute of Technology.

Kenstowicz, M. 1970. "On the Notation of Vowel Length in Lithuanian." *Papers in Linguistics* 3:73-114.

Kenstowicz, M. 1971. "Lithuanian Phonology." *Studies in the Linguistic Sciences.* 2:2, 1-85. Department of Linguistics. University of Illinois.

Kenstowicz, M. and J. Rubach. 1987. "The Phonology of Syllable Nuclei in Slovak." *Language* 63: 463-497.

Kiparsky, P. 1973. "The Inflectional Accent of Indo-European." *Language* 49:794-849.

Kiparsky, P. 1979. "Metrical Structure Assignment is Cyclic." *Linguistic Inquiry* 10:421-441.

Kiparsky, P. 1981. "Remarks on Metrical Structure of the Syllable." In Dressler, W. V., O. E. Pfeiffer, and J. R. Rennison (eds.), *Phonologica 80,* Proceedings of the Vienna International Conference on Phonology, Innsbruck, 245-256.

Kiparsky, P. 1982a. "Lexical Morphology and Phonology." In Yang, I. S. (ed.) *Linguistics in the Morning Calm*, 3-91. Seoul: Hanshin Publishing Co.

Kiparsky, P. 1982b. "From Cyclic Phonology to Lexical Phonology." In van der Hulst, H. and N. Smith (eds.) *The Structure of Phonological Representations.* Vol. 1: 131-175. Dordrecht: Foris Publications.

Kiparsky, P. 1983. "Word Formation and the Lexicon." In Ingemann, F. (ed.) *Proceedings of the 1982 Mid-America Linguistics Conference*, 3-29. Lawrence, Kansas: University of Kansas.

Kiparsky, P. 1984. "On the Lexical Phonology of Icelandic." Elert, C., I. Johansson, and E. Strangert (eds.) *Nordic Prosody III: Papers from a Symposium.* Umeå: University of Umeå.

Kiparsky, P. 1985. "Some Consequences of Lexical Phonology." In Ewen, C.J. and J.M. Anderson (eds.), *Phonology Yearbook* 2:85-138. Cambridge University Press.

Kiparsky, P. and M. Halle. 1977. "Towards a Reconstruction of the Indo- European Accent." In Hyman, L. (ed.) *Studies in Stress and Accent. Southern California Occasional Papers in Linguistics* 4:209-238. Los Angeles.

Lapointe, S. G. and M. H. Feinstein. 1984. "The Role of Vowel Deletion and Epenthesis in the Assignment of Syllable Structure." In van der Hulst, H. and N. Smith (eds.) *The Structure of Phonological Representation.* Vol. 2: 69-120. Dordrecht: Foris Publications.

Lehiste, I. and P. Ivić. 1967. "Some Problems Concerning the Syllable in Serbocroatian." *Glossa* 1/2:126-136.

Lehiste, I. and P. Ivić. 1986. *Word and Sentence Prosody in Serbocroatian.* Cambridge (Mass.): The MIT Press.

Lekach, A. F. 1979. "Phonological Markedness and the Sonority Hierarchy." In Safir, K. (ed.) *Papers on Syllable Structure, Metrical Structure and Harmony Processes. MIT Working Papers in Linguistics* 1:172- 177.

Leskien, A. 1914. *Grammatik der serbo-kroatischen Sprache.* Heidelberg: Carl Winter's Universitätsbuchhandlung.

Leskien, A. 1975 [1885, 1893]. "Untersuchungen über Quantität und Betonung in den slavischen Sprachen." In *Slavische und Baltische Forschungen.* Part 1. Leipzig: Zentralantiquariat der DDR.

Levin, J. 1985. *A Metrical Theory of Syllabicity.* Doctoral Dissertation. Massachusetts Institute of Technology.

Liberman, A. 1982. *The Scandinavian Languages.* Minneapolis: University of Minnesota Press.

Liberman, M. and A. Prince. 1977. "On Stress and Linguistic Rhythm." *Linguistic Inquiry* 8:249-336.

Lightner, T. M. 1972. *Russian Phonology and Turkish Phonology. Problems in the Theory of Phonology.* Edmonton, Alberta: Linguistic Research, Inc.

Matešić, J. 1970. *Der Wortakzent in der serbokroatischen Schriftssprache.* Heidelberg: Carl Winter Universitätsverlag.

McCarthy, J. 1979a. "On Stress and Syllabification." *Linguistic Inquiry* 10:443-465.

McCarthy, J. 1979b. *Formal Problems in Semitic Phonology and Morphology.* Doctoral Dissertation. Massachusetts Institute of Technology.

McCarthy, J. 1988. "Feature geometry and dependency: a review." *Phonetica* 45.2: 84-108.

McCarthy, J. and A. Prince. 1986. *Prosodic Morphology.* Unpublished manuscript, University of Massachussets at Amherst.

Mohanan, K.P. 1982. *Lexical Phonology.* Doctoral Dissertation. Massachusetts Institute of Technology.

Mohanan, K.P. 1986. *The Theory of Lexical Phonology.* Dordrecht: Reidel.

Nespor, M. and I. Vogel. 1982. "Prosodic Domains of External Sandhi Rules." In van der Hulst, H. and N. Smith (eds.) *The Structure of Phonological Representations.* Part 2. Dordrecht: Foris Publications.

Nespor, M. and I. Vogel. 1986. *Prosodic Phonology*. Dordrecht: Foris Publications.

Nikolić, B. M. 1970. *Osnovi mladje novoštokavske akcentuacije*. Beograd: Institut za Srpskohrvatski jezik.

Poser, W.J. 1984a. "Hypocoristic Formation in Japanese." In Cobler, M., S. MacKaye and M. T. Wescoat (eds.), *Proceedings of the Third West Coast Conference on Formal Linguistics*, 218-229. Stanford Linguistics Association

Poser, W.J. 1984b. *The Phonetics and Phonology of Tone and Intonation in Japanese* Doctoral Dissertation. Massachusetts Institute of Technology.

Poser, W.J. 1990. "Evidence for Foot Structure in Japanese." *Language* 66:78-105.

Prince, A.S. 1983. "Relating to the Grid." Linguistic Inquiry 14: 19-100.

Prince, A.S. 1985. "Improving Tree Theory." In Proceedings of the Berkeley Linguistics Society 11, Berkeley Linguistics Society, Berkeley, 471-490.

Pulleyblank, D. 1983. *Tone in Lexical Phonology*. Doctoral Dissertation. Massachusetts Institute of Technology.

Pulleyblank, D. 1986. *Tone in Lexical Phonology*. Dordrecht: Reidel.

Rubach, J. 1984. *Cyclic and Lexical Phonology*. Dordrecht: Foris Publications.

Sagey, E. 1986. *The Representation of Features and Relations in Non-Linear Phonology*. Doctoral Dissertation. Massachusetts Institute of Technology.

Scatton, E. A. 1975. *Bulgarian Phonology*. Cambridge (Mass.): Slavica Publishers.

Scatton, E. A. 1984. *A Reference Grammar of Modern Bulgarian*. Columbus: Slavica Publishers.

Schein, B. and D. Steriade. 1986. "On Geminates." *Linguistic Inquiry* 17:691-744.

Selkirk, E. O. 1978. "On Prosodic Structure and its Relation to Syntactic Structure." In Fretheim, T. (ed.) *Nordic Prosody II.* Trondheim: TAPIR.

Selkirk, E. O. 1980. "The Role of Prosodic Categories in English Word Stress." *Linguistic Inquiry* 11:563-605.

Selkirk, E. O. 1981. "Epenthesis and Degenerate Syllables in Cairene Arabic." In Borer, H. and Y. Aoun (eds.) *Theoretical Issues in the Grammar of Semitic Languages.* MIT Working Papers in Linguistics 3:209-232.

Selkirk, E. O. 1982. "The Syllable." In van der Hulst, H. and N. Smith (eds.) *The Structure of Phonological Representations.* Part II. Dordrecht: Foris Publications.

Selkirk, E. O. 1984a. "On the Major Class Features and the Syllable Theory." Aronoff, M. and R. Oehrle (eds.) *Language Sound Structure.* Cambridge (Mass.): The MIT Press.

Selkirk, E. O. 1984b. *Phonology and Syntax.* Cambridge (Mass.): The MIT Press.

Selkirk, E. O. 1986. "On Derived Domains in Sentence Phonology." In Ewen, C. J. and J. M. Anderson (eds.), *Phonology Yearbook 3*, 371-405.

Senn, A. 1966. *Handbuch der litauischen Sprache.* I. Heidelberg: Carl Winter.

Shieber, S. M. 1986. *An Introduction to Unification-Based Approaches to Grammar.* Stanford: Center for the Study of Language and Information.

Steriade, D. 1982. *Greek Prosodies and the Nature of Syllabification.* Doctoral Dissertation. Massachusetts Institute of Technology.

Steriade, D. 1988. Review of *CV Phonology* by G. Clements and S. Keyser. *Language* 64:118-129.

Stowell, T. 1979. "Stress Systems of the World, Unite!" In Safir, K. (ed.) *Papers on Syllable Structure, Metrical Structure and Harmony Processes*. MIT Working Papers in Linguistics 1:51-76.

Street, J.C. 1963. *Khalkha Structure*. Uralic and Altaic Series, Vol. 24. Bloomington, Indiana.

Trubetzkoy, N. S. 1969 [1939]. *Principles of Phonology*. Translated by C. A. M. Baltaxe. University of California Press: Berkeley and Los Angeles.

Vogel, I. 1977. *The Syllable in Phonological Theory with Special Reference to Italian*. Doctoral Dissertation. Stanford University.

Zec, D. 1988. "Bulgarian ə Epenthesis: A Case for Moraic Structure." In Blevins, J. and J. Carter (eds.), *Proceedings of the Eighteenth Annual Meeting of the North Eastern Linguistic Society*, Vol. 2:553-566. University of Massachusetts, Amherst.

Zec, D. and S. Inkelas. 1987. "Phonological Phrasing and the Reduction of Function Words." Paper presented at the 62nd Meeting of the Linguistic Society of America, San Francisco, CA.

Index

adjunction, 17, 39, 40, 42, 47, 48, 59, 81, 88, 101, 124
Aklan, 17, 43
Arabic, Cairene, 17, 43

Berber, Imdlawn Tashlhiyt, 40, 43
  emphatic articulation, 42
  syllabic consonants in, 40–42
Bulgarian, 7, 89–94, 98, 100, 102, 103, 105–108, 110–113, 115, 186
  Epenthesis, 83
  Final Devoicing, 94–98
  liquid metathesis, 90, 91
  moraic segments in, 100, 101, 106
  Yer Delinking, 93–95, 99, 102, 105, 106, 110, 111, 115
  Yer Vocalization, 92, 93, 115

Cheremis, Eastern, 188
Chinese, 9
Chukchee, 67, 68
clitic group, 96, 97, 110
consonant
  moraic, 16, 19, 38, 47, 48, 50, 52, 55, 60, 80, 82
  syllabic, 22, 34, 40–42, 60, 187, 188

Danish, 19–22, 34, 39, 43

stød, 19–21, 59
Stød Linking, 21, 59
diphthong, 114

English, 14, 15, 17, 43, 47, 48, 59, 70, 78, 81, 110, 161, 188

foot, 4, 38, 44, 108
  moraic, 125, 126
  sonority requirements on, 187, 188

geminate, 180
geminates, 9, 19, 40
Greek, 70, 71

Hausa, 110
Hebrew, Tiberian, 14

Ilocano, 52
Italian, 19, 38, 39, 69

Japanese, 39, 130, 181, 184

Klamath, 67, 68
Kwakwala, 19, 32, 36, 39, 43, 47–49, 55, 56, 61, 80, 81
  glottalized sonorants, 33, 36, 37, 48, 67, 69
  metrical structure, 36
  moraic sonorants in, 34, 36, 37

reduplication, 33
stress, 34, 38

Latin, 70, 85, 86
lexical component, 3, 5, 25, 26, 42, 90, 92, 96, 100, 112, 129, 130, 132
lexical level, 3, 5, 7, 89, 100, 112, 113, 130, 133, 170
   cyclic, 3, 92, 93, 99–101, 105, 110–112, 131, 133, 145, 159
   postcyclic, 3, 92, 94, 99, 100, 102, 112, 133
lexical phonology and morphology, 3, 5, 90
Lithuanian, 19, 22, 23, 25, 26, 39, 130
   Ablaut, 26–30
   accent retraction, 23, 24
   moraic sonorants in, 22–25
   Nasal Infixation, 26, 29–32, 60
   Nonfinal Lengthening, 32

metrical structure, subsyllabic, 5, 6, 8, 62, 184
Mongolian, Khalkha, 18, 43
mora, 3–8, 10
   as primitive, 5, 7–9, 11, 12, 52, 56–59
   head, 45, 101, 123, 133, 135, 169, 181, 187, 188
   nonhead, 27, 181
   sonority requirements on, 7, 11, 81, 103, 104, 107, 187
   strong, 45, 84, 169
   weak, 84
morification, 7, 62, 78–80, 84, 85, 88, 113, 122, 123

obstruent
   moraic, 14, 40
   syllabic, 40, 47, 50

Pali, 87

phonological word, 4, 92, 95–98, 108, 110, 112, 135, 185–187
   lexical, 96–99, 110
   postlexical, 97, 99, 110
Polish, 96
postlexical component, 3, 25, 30, 32, 95
prosodic hierarchy, 3–5, 96, 97, 107–110, 184, 185, 187
   morphosyntactically based, 186, 187
   sonority-based, 187
prosodic licensing, 4, 5, 7, 8, 90, 100, 101, 108, 110, 184
prosodic structure, 3–5, 7, 77, 89, 90, 93, 100, 101, 107, 108, 126, 166, 189

rules
   cyclic, 3, 92, 110, 115, 118, 123, 130, 132, 133, 135, 145, 167, 175
   lexical, 3, 21, 92, 94–99, 110, 128–130, 133, 145, 181
   noncyclic, 3
   postcyclic, 3, 92, 94, 98, 100, 110, 128, 129, 132–135, 144, 164
   postlexical, 32, 60, 96, 118, 181

Sanskrit, 71, 130
Seneca, 60
Serbo-Croatian, 7, 105, 111–118, 121, 123, 126–128, 130, 132, 133, 159, 171, 180
   Initial High Insertion, 129, 130, 135, 143, 144, 153–156, 164, 167
   Metatony, 168–170, 174, 175
   moraic segments in, 83, 114
   pitch accent, 112, 113, 127–129, 132, 135, 143, 156,

157, 161, 165, 171, 173, 176–178, 181–183
presonorant lengthening, 113–115, 118, 120–123, 160, 165, 167, 170, 180
Stem Truncation, 172–175, 177, 178
stress, 127, 129, 178
Tonal Node Assignment, 134, 135, 160, 166, 168
Tone Linking, 130–140, 142–145, 147, 148, 150–156, 160–164, 166–171, 174–179
Tone Spreading, 128–130, 133–135, 138, 148–152, 162–164, 174, 181
Yer Delinking, 118, 122–124, 165, 167, 168, 170, 182
Yer Vocalization, 117, 118, 123

sonorant
  moraic, 18, 21, 22, 24, 25, 34, 48, 82, 114, 121, 122, 124
  syllabic, 18
sonority
  major class features and, 63, 64, 68, 75, 87
  minimal distance, 70–73, 86
  ranking, 64–66, 69–76, 87
  scale, 13–15, 40, 49, 52, 57, 59, 62–71, 73, 74, 77, 86, 87
  sequencing, 70, 84
Strict Layer Hypothesis, 4, 5, 8, 108, 109, 186
Strong Domain Hypothesis, 111, 113, 130, 180
syllabification, 7, 10, 41, 42, 62, 64, 77, 81, 83, 84, 89, 98, 99, 102, 110, 113–115, 122–124, 180, 186
syllable
  bimoraic, 12, 17–20, 25, 29, 34, 46, 48, 83, 84, 107, 128
  closed, 7, 11, 14, 16–20, 22, 24, 25, 29–32, 35, 37, 38, 46–52, 54, 55, 60, 61, 80, 81, 103, 105
  coda, 19–21, 30, 31, 38–40, 42, 48, 53, 54, 56, 57, 59–61, 98
  contact, 84, 85
  heavy, 7, 11–14, 16–20, 22, 31, 32, 34, 35, 38, 43, 44, 46, 47, 49–55, 60, 61, 106
  light, 12–14, 16, 18, 19, 32, 34, 35, 37, 46, 47, 49, 53–55, 60, 61, 81, 82, 106
  monomoraic, 17, 18, 34, 81, 82, 102, 103, 107
  nucleus, 13, 42, 46, 54, 56, 57, 59, 61, 64, 84, 110
  onset, 6, 9, 11, 31, 38, 52, 59, 60
  open, 17, 18, 25, 35
  peak, 14, 40, 42, 44, 64, 65, 83, 88, 103, 107
  rhyme, 6, 9, 52, 54–56, 59
  sonority requirements on, 6, 7, 11, 45, 46, 57, 62, 70, 104, 187, 188
  trimoraic (superheavy), 25, 26, 28–32, 59

Trubetzkoy's generalization, 7, 52

underspecification, 74, 128

vowel
  diphthong, 18, 27, 29, 83, 111, 185
  long, 17, 18, 20, 22, 25, 26, 28, 31–35, 51, 60, 61, 83, 113, 114, 124–126, 128, 131, 135, 137, 138, 140, 145, 149, 151, 152, 155,

167, 173, 175, 178, 180, 182, 183, 185
moraic, 14, 18, 34, 47, 50, 82, 114
short, 17, 18, 20, 25–28, 31, 41, 47, 125, 135, 136, 140, 141, 145, 152, 160, 167, 170, 173, 176
yer, 92–94, 98, 102, 104–107, 110, 111, 115–118, 120–124, 160, 165–170, 180, 182

Yidin^y, 14

For Product Safety Concerns and Information please contact our EU
representative GPSR@taylorandfrancis.com
Taylor & Francis Verlag GmbH, Kaufingerstraße 24, 80331 München, Germany

www.ingramcontent.com/pod-product-compliance
Lightning Source LLC
Chambersburg PA
CBHW052113300426
44116CB00010B/1653